The Nile Campaign, 1884–1885

The Letters and Sketches of Rudolph de Lisle RN

Lieutenant Rudolph M.P. de Lisle (1853–1885). Taken *c.*1884, a year before his death at the Battle of Abu Klea 17 January 1885.

The Nile Campaign, 1884–1885

The Letters and Sketches of Rudolph de Lisle RN

Gerard de Lisle FSA

Pen & Sword
MILITARY

First published in Great Britain in 2024 by
Pen & Sword Military
An imprint of Pen & Sword Books Limited
Yorkshire – Philadelphia
In association with The Garendon Press, Leicestershire

ISBN 978 1 39905 836 0

A CIP catalogue record for this book is
available from the British Library

Typeset by Mac Style
Printed and bound in India by Parksons Graphics Pvt. Ltd.

Pen & Sword Books Limited incorporates the imprints of After the Battle, Atlas, Archaeology, Aviation, Discovery, Family History, Fiction, History, Maritime, Military, Military Classics, Politics, Select, Transport, True Crime, Air World, Frontline Publishing, Leo Cooper, Remember When, Seaforth Publishing, The Praetorian Press, Wharncliffe Local History, Wharncliffe Transport, Wharncliffe True Crime and White Owl.

For a complete list of Pen & Sword titles please contact

PEN & SWORD BOOKS LIMITED
47 Church Street, Barnsley, South Yorkshire, S70 2AS, England
E-mail: enquiries@pen-and-sword.co.uk
Website: www.pen-and-sword.co.uk
or
PEN AND SWORD BOOKS
1950 Lawrence Rd, Havertown, PA 19083, USA
E-mail: uspen-and-sword@casematepublishers.com
Website: www.penandswordbooks.com

Contents

Rudolph de Lisle's Nile Medal

Rudolph's Nile Medal, presented posthumously to his mother, Laura de Lisle.

Accoutrements of Rudolph de Lisle RN

Epaulettes & Hat – 8245.

Box (Closed) – 8204.

Maker's Label – 8208.

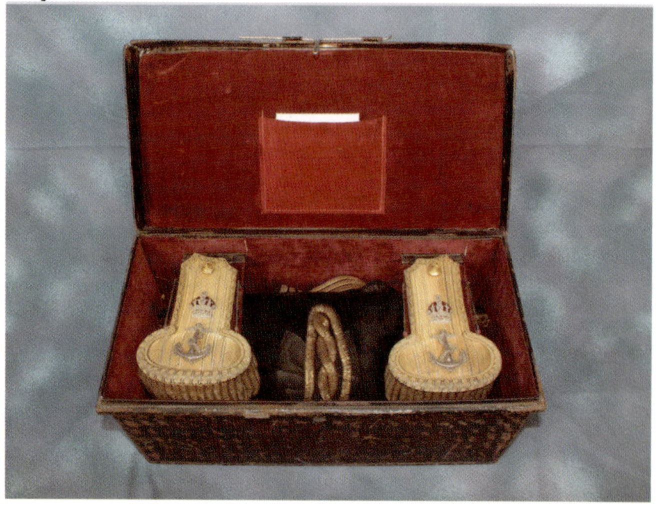

Box (Open) – 8261.

Rudolph's Monogram – 8209.

Rudolph's Epaulettes, Bicorn Hat, and Sword Belt, in original, monogrammed Gieve Matthews and Seagrove Ltd box. Purchased Hamburg, Germany, in 2021 through the agency of Herr Une Hoppe, NATO friend of Col. Hubert de Lisle.

Swords

Victorian Naval Officer Sword – Rudolph de Lisle (1853–1885).

Edwardan Naval Officer Sword – Rudolph de Lisle (1892–1943).

Edwardian Naval Officer Dirk – Rudolph de Lisle (1892–1943).

The three swords acquired from the Hon. Mrs Everard (Mary Rose) de Lisle, February 2021.

To all at Pen and Sword

Introduction & Acknowledgements

I am thrilled that this volume is being published by Pen & Sword as it is the last set of sketches and watercolours by Lt. Rudolph de Lisle RN, who died heroically at the Battle of Abu Klea on 17 January 1885.

The Hon. Mary Rose de Lisle has generously given me a hoard of very special items of Rudolph's, and it is my privilege to edit the best of these in two volumes.

In effect this is to commemorate not only a very brave naval officer but also a great English gentleman; known for his gentleness but also for his fair use of discipline.

The previous volume about the Peruvian-Chilean War 1879–1881 was published by Pen & Sword in 2008 and was translated into Spanish and published in Peru in 2022. Therefore, yet again I am most grateful to Brigadier Henry Wilson for his encouragement in producing this tome. A further volume – also by Pen & Sword – relating to Rudolph's world-wide voyages will follow in the fullness of time.

I am extremely grateful to Mr David Howell for allowing me to reproduce his masterly article on Rudolph which he published in 'Soldiers of the Queen', the *Journal of the Victorian Military Society*, Issue 116, Autumn-Winter 2016.

I also wish to thank Mr James Caverhill ACR for expertly conserving the weather-beaten sketch book of Rudolph's ascent of the Nile which has permitted the best of these invaluable testimonies to be reproduced here.

I have also received patient help with tracing reproductions of Rudolph's watercolours in *The Illustrated London News*; I am most grateful to the staff over many years.

To Mr David Edwards for being our assiduous family photographer for over 50 years and who has now made valiant efforts to reproduce these sketches and watercolours as near to the originals as possible. Regrettably, some of the pencil sketches have faded with the test of time.

Innumerable friends, acquaintances, learned persons and institutions have provided data and titbits for my research and all these items – welded together like a giant jigsaw – have allowed me to complete this tome, which has been pending over many years, but which (at last) will soon be seeing the light of day.

And, finally, my long-suffering assistant, Lorren Boniface, for her patience in transcribing, typing, re-typing, copy-editing and proof-reading the drafts, hunting down references, creating the genealogy, checking the additional notes, and preparing the index.

Naturally any errors are my responsibility. I would welcome any comments and especially any further information to fill the gaps left blank, or to explain the paucity of data for some of the entries and footnotes.

Gerard de Lisle
Cold Newton Lodge
January 2024

HMS *Alexandra*. Rudolph's sketch of HMS *Alexandra*, reproduced in H.N. Oxenham's *Memoir of Lieutenant Rudolph de Lisle R.N.*

Exculpation

In transcribing Rudolph's letters, we have chosen to reproduce the original language in full. Readers should be aware that Rudolph was a man of his time and, as such, on occasion he uses terms reflective of that period that are totally unacceptable today. We apologise for any offence or distress reading such language might cause.

Gerard de Lisle
Cold Newton Lodge
January 2024

A Leicestershire Naval Officer

The Life and Early Death of Lieutenant Rudolph Edward Lisle March Phillipps de Lisle RN, 1853–1885

David Howell

'When Allah made the Sudan, he laughed.'
(Old Arab proverb)

Rudolph Edward Lisle March Phillipps de Lisle was born at Gracedieu Manor,[1] Leicestershire, on 23 November 1853, the penultimate youngest son and the fourteenth child of Ambrose and Laura March Phillipps de Lisle, he had seven sisters and eight brothers in total. Ambrose de Lisle had converted to Roman Catholicism, was the author of several devotional works, an extensive landowner and had adopted the de Lisle name in right of his grandmother, Susan Lisle, the last of her line. Rudolph was baptized on the day of his birth in the family chapel and his sponsors were the 8th Earl of Denbigh and Lady Edward Fitzalan Howard.

The original Phillipps family line having died out when the last direct male descendant died in 1774, the estates were inherited through the female line and marriage, eventually passing to Ambrose March Phillipps de Lisle of Gracedieu and Garendon.[2] Rudolph was only four when his elder brother Everard was killed at the siege of Delhi during the mutiny of 1857 and subsequently awarded the Victoria Cross.[3]

Described as 'an engaging, fair-haired child in a red cassock and surplice serving as an acolyte'[4] in the family chapel at Gracedieu, Rudolph was also described by his nurse in 1886 as 'a truthful child always frank and open', prompt to acknowledge any wrongdoing but with a predisposition to a hasty temper and violent passion. It was during childhood holidays in Whitby that he first expressed a love of the sea and things nautical which would shape his future life.

In 1864 Rudolph's father Ambrose gave up Gracedieu in favour of his eldest son, also named Ambrose, and prepared to move to Garendon Hall then undergoing refurbishment. During the interim, of 18 months, home became Longcliffe

---

1. Grace Dieu Manor originally an Augustinian Priory built c.1240 but suppressed in 1538. Later, passing through the Beaumonts, it was sold to the Phillipps family in 1690.
2. Garendon, *c.*1133 originally a Cistercian Monastery, dissolved in 1536. Built as a house in the mid-seventeenth century and rebuilt in the Palladian style in the mid-eighteenth century.
3. Everard Aloysius Lisle March Phillipps VC (1835–1857), 11th Bengal Native Infantry and 60th Rifles. See Leicestershire Historian 2014.
4. The Rev. H.N. Oxenham (1829–1888), a Catholic scholar and controversialist. A Master at Harrow who wrote a biography of Rudolph.

Grace Dieu Manor, Rudolph's childhood home: 1856 sketch by Baigent; *c*.1930 photocard; and present day (overleaf).

in the Charnwood Forest, where Rudolph learnt to shoot and began to demonstrate his ability to draw and sketch picturesque views.

When he was 12 years old he joined his elder brothers Osmund, Frank and Edwin at Oscott College.[5] Christmas 1865 was spent with the family at Garendon Hall and he returned to Oscott for six months, then took a two month break before his enrolment as a Naval Cadet.

On 1 October 1866, Rudolph de Lisle, not yet 13, was taken by his older brother Osmund to The Royal Naval and Military Academy, Gosport[6] to prepare for the Training Ship *Britannia*.[7] He was now set upon the path for a career in the Royal Navy.

There were 90 other boys enrolled with him, none of whom were of the same faith, but within three weeks he had settled down to naval life and his studies. The headmaster, the Rev. Edward Burney, wrote to his parents: 'We are very much pleased with him, his general conduct is exemplary.' This was followed by others in a similar vein – 'a most amiable, good boy' – and the Headmaster had expectations of him taking a 'first class' when he left *Britannia*. As the only Roman Catholic he spent his Sundays with a local priest, Dr Baldaconi, an Italian at the Catholic Mission Gosport and, as with

5. Oscott College, a Roman Catholic College established in 1836 at Sutton Coldfield, north of Birmingham.
6. A reference to Burneys Naval Military Academy 1791–1904. Later granted a 'Royal' prefix by Queen Victoria.
7. Naval College and *Britannia* a training ship from 1859–1903. Built in 1820 a three decker, replaced in 1866.

Dr Burney, Rudolph de Lisle had made an excellent impression. 'The Angel of the Congregation' was Baldaconi's summation.

The journey from 13-year-old schoolboy with elder brothers to protect him at Oscott to life as one of 90 other cadets in a naval dormitory cannot have been easy but clearly he settled to it well. Oxenham in his biography of de Lisle states that the conversations in the night time dormitory were 'repulsive to one brought up as he had been', and de Lisle remedied this by reading tales from *The Arabian Nights*, which is difficult to imagine but then de Lisle's biographer presented a somewhat aureate picture of him perhaps uncommon in a military establishment then or now.

De Lisle spent Christmas 1866 at Garendon with his family and returned to Gosport on 7 January 1867 to prepare for the impending examination. On 9 April he passed out sixth in his class, of the 65 applicants, transferring to HMS *Britannia* on 2 May and remaining till July 1868. In a letter home he writes of his worry that some initiation ceremony involving an anchor tattoo and gunpowder was likely to be performed on his arm 'but that it did not matter as it would not be seen'.

Rudolph at 8 years old.

During periods of leave he visited his relative Lord Clifford at Ugbrooke Park[8] in Chudleigh, Devon, or on occasion spent a weekend with an uncle then in his seventies, Henry Cranmer March Phillipps in Torquay.[9] De Lisle made many friends on *Britannia* to whom he wrote long after they were all dispersed on the high seas, one in particular was Lord Maurice Fitzgerald[10] a second son of the Duke of Leinster. Before he left *Britannia* the sponsor at his baptism, Lord Denbigh, wrote to him offering a presentation sword with engraved de Lisle coat of arms, initials and the motto '*Pugno pro Deo patria Justitia*'. De Lisle accepted the gift and wore this sword until the last day of his life and service.[11]

In July 1868 he joined his family at Garendon and was seen there by his biographer the Rev. Oxenham 'as a boy … that lithe and graceful frame and face singularly beautiful … sun crowned with a lustrous purity of spirit' which, even allowing for a Victorian clergyman's hyperbole, seems a trifle florid! At the end of the month de Lisle joined

8. Mentioned in *Domesday*, Ugbrooke Park has been the home of the Cliffords since 1604.
9. H.C.M. Phillipps (1793–1880) JP of Wellswood Hall, a plaque in Torquay records that Phillipps in 1873 threw himself into the sea to rescue and save a drowning child.
10. (1852–1901). Son of the 4th duke, the family home was at Kilkea Castle, Co Kildare.
11. 'I fight for God, my Country and for what is Right.'

Garendon Hall, ancestral home of the March Phillipps de Lisle family.

HMS *Victory*, by then permanently moored at Portsmouth. This was not a lengthy posting as on 2 September he joined HMS *Bristol* as a sub lieutenant[12] destined for the Mediterranean.

On 8 September the *Bristol* moved to Plymouth and at 0700 hrs that day de Lisle fell overboard into the water, rose up and was rescued by a boat, little the worse for his ducking. The *Bristol* sailed for Gibraltar on 10 September and after 'a very rough passage' arrived there on the 27th. Almost immediately the ship was ordered off to Malaga where a popular revolt was threatening British interests.[13] De Lisle was impressed by the beauty of Spain and Malaga but described the Spanish as 'looking like a set of cut-throats' and some much worse. His artistic skills were not utilised as he had wished to produce water colours of The Rock but had managed to paint four watercolours on the sea journey down.

The ship was stood down from Spain after a couple of days and returned to Gibraltar only to be ordered to Malta shortly after. Accepting that de Lisle was 15 years old his comments about the Maltese even exceeded those on the

12. In the nineteenth century a Passed Midshipman was eligible for promotion once a vacancy became available. By 1861 this rank had been abolished and sub-Lieutenant was instituted.

13. In 1866 a lengthy revolt resulted in Queen Isabella fleeing Spain and the formation of the 1st Spanish Republic in 1873.

Spaniards, 'the most brutal scoundrels that ever existed', but were hardly based on wide experience. More likely it was a repeated observation from the Officers' wardroom.

His naval duties in the Mediterranean, Italy and Algiers kept him away from home and England for nearly twelve months but on arrival at Plymouth he was granted two days leave in May 1869 before being drafted onto HMS *Barrosa* sailing from Plymouth on 19 June 1869. He was in a flying squadron, a flotilla of six ships destined for those far-flung outposts of the empire and to relieve ships at various stations. It was a lengthy tour about which de Lisle waxed enthusiastically for the picturesque scenes, people and colours he had witnessed – but was less enthusiastic about the food, 'nothing but salt horse and biscuit for dinner, salt pork (like shoe leather) being extra salted for the hot weather, tea without milk and biscuit for breakfast and tea and only on Sundays any fresh meat'.

On 23 November 1870, at the end of a stormy passage from the Cape of Good Hope to Melbourne, he attained his 16th birthday but a month later on Christmas Eve as he was preparing to attend a ball he received the devastating news of his brother Osmund's death, which affected him deeply, writing 'a new leaf has been turned over'. He wrote considerably on his grief at the loss of his brother but also on the death of a fellow midshipman who fell overboard from HMS *Scylla* whilst they were crossing the Pacific.

When his ship put into Yokohama at Easter 1870 he returned to HMS *Liverpool* and arrived back in Plymouth Sound on 15 November. The Liverpool crew were paid off on 2 December and de Lisle returned home to Garendon for Christmas and a four-month period of leave.

After his leave he first joined HMS *Himalaya* and then HMS *Cameleon*[14] in 1871 for a lengthy tour of duty in the Pacific. He received two promotions during 1874, the first in May to Acting Lieutenant aboard HMS *Scout* and again to Acting Lieutenant on HMS *Cameleon* in December, where he remained until returning home in May 1875.

This was followed by a course at The Naval College, Greenwich, passing all examinations and obtaining his certificate for Lieutenant. In July 1876 he returned to the Mediterranean Squadron serving on HMS *Sultan* until October 1879. During the next two years de Lisle was again in the Pacific on HMS *Shannon* where he witnessed at close hand the war between Peru and Chile. The UK was not an active protagonist in the war, but de Lisle was able to keenly observe events, keep a diary and painted a number of watercolours depicting scenes from the conflict.[15] His letters home contain considerable and enjoyable detail about his travels and observations as well as the accounts of more lively events in the war of the two states which ended in 1880 with the capture and burning of Lima. He recounts that he and other English officers had carried water and wine to wounded soldiers who had been left for two days without food or water on a battlefield. In an age when political correctness was not a factor de Lisle also continued in the vein of making acerbic comments about the Roman Catholic Clergy of the South Americas that were far from complimentary. This did not extend to three young American females who were invited to join him and his shipmates for an impromptu party and dance at 9am one morning whilst they were waiting for a train. They were on their way to climb a nearby mountain in Peru at 17,000 ft on the lower end of the Andes.[16]

---

14. HMS *Himalaya* purchased by the Royal Navy from P&O in 1854 serving until 1920. HMS *Cameleon* launched in 1860 and sold in 1883, one of several ships of that name from 1777–1960.
15. *The Royal Navy and the Peruvian Chilean War 1879–1881. Rudolph de Lisle's Diary & Watercolours.* Published by Pen and Sword Books, 176pp with watercolours and edited by Gerard de Lisle, Rudolph's great nephew.
16. This mountain is referred to as 'Mt Meigs' Peru. The name has evidently changed but remains unidentified.

His Pacific travels lasted until June 1881 when after landing at Devonport he enjoyed a few days with his mother in her new home at Onebarrow, Leicestershire, where she had moved to from Garendon Hall after the marriage of her eldest son. He also visited his two sisters in Atherstone, Warwickshire, and France. On 3 October 1881 he returned to Plymouth and joined HMS *Vernon* briefly before commencing a torpedo and gunnery course at the Royal Naval College Greenwich until July the following year. The Christmas of that year was the last one he would spend with his mother and four surviving brothers: during the next two years two of his brothers, Frank and the eldest Ambrose, were to pre-decease him.

By November 1882 he was serving on HMS *Excellent* and managed a visit to his mother and a sister, but in the middle of January 1883 he took what was to prove his final farewell from them at Garendon Hall. They were never to see him again.

He travelled to Gibraltar and joined his final ship HMS *Alexandra* moving on to Malta, the Adriatic and Greek Islands as well as Montenegro and Dalmatia. Further jaunts around the Mediterranean continued as the Royal Navy policed the seas and British Empire and at a stop in Famagusta at the Cathedral he found the tomb of a Crusader Sire John de l'Ile whom de Lisle claimed as an ancestor. Shortly after this visit he was in Port Said describing the hot winds of the desert, just like a blast out of a furnace which caused him to have his head shaved as though he had 'returned from penal servitude'.

Rudolph, aged 27, taken in 1880 at the famous Courret Hermanos Studio, Lima, Peru.

Events in Egypt[17] during 1881–2 had committed British forces to support the Ottoman empire and Khedive of Egypt to quell the Arabi rebellion which was no sooner dealt with than a greater threat emerged as Khartoum was besieged by a new religious leader, the Mahdi[18] who had already been very successful defeating the Egyptian forces of the Khedive[19] and had seized their armaments.

The British were now committed to further conflict to prop up the Khedive, and in 1884 sent General Charles George Gordon[20] to Khartoum to organise an evacuation. Even before becoming fully involved de Lisle was critical of the Government's stance on both Egypt and Sudan. In August 1884 his ship received orders to ascend the Nile and assist Gordon in the relief of Khartoum.

---

17. Colonel Achmed Arabi led a rebellion 1879–1882 against Turkish rule in Egypt which was crushed with major assistance from the British. Arabi was exiled to Ceylon.
18. The Mahdi Mohammed Ahmed (1843–1885) was born of lowly parents but well educated. His name and that of his parents coincided with a prophecy that Islam would be regenerated by a force of arms led by the Mahdi (The Guided One). The prophecy was set for 1300 Mohammedan era (1883 AD).
19. Khedive. A Turkish rank equivalent to Viceroy. A Khedive ruled Egypt as a vassal state until the Ottoman Empire was defeated and collapsed in 1918.
20. Charles 'Chinese' Gordon 1833–1885 a Royal Engineer officer who had previously governed Khartoum and southern Sudan in 1877 under the Khedives Ishmael and Tewfik but had resigned in 1880.

In what must be viewed as a prescient twist, and the first example of 'privatisation', Thomas Cook and Sons, the Leicester-founded travel company, were appointed as contractors to provide support to the Army. Arrangements were made for the company to transport 18,000 troops, nearly 40,000 tons of supplies, 40,000 tons of coal and 800 whaleboats. To transport the coal from Tyneside to Boulac and Assiout via Alexandria, 28 large steamers and 6,000 railway trucks were required. An additional 7,000 railway trucks were needed for the military stores, while on the Nile 27 steamers and 650 sailing boats were used to carry the troops and supplies all of which relied on the labour of 5,000 local men and boys. Troops were moved up the Nile by steamboats towing 800 whalers in long lines. Cook and Sons were contracted originally to transport only up the Nile as far as Waidi Haifa[21] and needless to say there was the usual bureaucratic muddle and arguments over contracts and costs, but the War Office later gave Thomas Cook 'great credit … for the satisfactory way in which your contract was performed'. Some journalists ventured to say later that had the whole expedition been transported by Cook's Tours to Khartoum it might have been more successful! The contract was managed by John Mason Cook[22] from Cook & Sons' Cairo office.

Also utilised were 300 Canadian 'voyageurs', a class of 'river steersmen' whom Wolseley had previously employed during the Red River rebellion of 1877 and whose 'endurance and efficiency he never forgot'.[23]

De Lisle provides a detailed narrative of his adventures in a series of letters written to his mother commencing on 15 August 1884 from his ship off the port of Alexandria. The first letter sets out that he believed the Royal Navy had been given a tough job as the Army had 'declared the task impossible' and that the Admiral had informed him that 'sometimes what others thought impossible the navy did not'. De Lisle had been selected with other officers and men from HMS *Alexandra*, *Inflexible*, *Iris*, *Monarch*, *Superb*, and *Temeraire* to help move the Army upriver towards Khartoum, but in a further letter on 19 August he expressed continued doubts about the rushed time scales[24] and physical demands of getting all the boats and men over the eighteen Nile cataracts: 'If only the government could have made their minds up six weeks or two months earlier but the future only is before us and few know what it may bring.'

Despite his misgivings on the task he was able to indulge in some sightseeing in Luxor and Assouan (Aswan) and had to take responsibility for the punishment of a recalcitrant seaman who had broken into a wine store. By 18 September he was at the second cataract and bemoaning the Nile's width, depth, the heat, the speed of the water over the cataracts, and the loss of two pairs of boots which had succumbed to the sharp gravel and granite rock. On 1 November he was writing from 'The Camp of the Naval Brigade, Sarras' and mentions having sent his will 'which I trust is not necessary just yet, but may be.'

By then the river had dropped and he had a camel ride of 50 miles to inspect some 'bad places' further upstream. In a later letter he described this trip as a very pleasant one despite finding one of the ships the *Ghizeh*, wrecked near Tanjur but the crew safe. He mentions from camp that he was one of three Royal Navy Officers, with a Boatswain and

21. Waidi Haifa – known to the troops as 'bloody halfway'.
22. (1834–1899). 'The King of Egypt' a sobriquet given to him by the Egyptians on account of his generous 'baksheesh'.
23. The steersmen were recruited and led by Frederick Charles Denison, a former Militia Officer and Toronto Lawyer. The consensus after the unsuccessful campaign was that the voyageurs were 'a most pronounced success' which was endorsed by John Mason Cook son of the founder who had initially raised doubts about their use and had favoured the use of Egyptian boatmen.
24. The Gladstone Government had delayed the decision about the relief of Khartoum and the rescue of Gordon until it was too late and suffered much public opprobrium particularly when news of his death arrived in the UK.

45 Bluejackets, two stokers, two engine room artificers, a carpenter and an Egyptian interpreter, who had charge of one Gardner Machine Gun and 8,000 rounds of ammunition. The River Nile also claimed casualties, including 28 men drowned, six of whom were the Canadian voyageurs.

His next three letters did not reach his family until after his death but he mentions that his drawings for the *Illustrated London News* had been published in his letter of 6 January 1885. In this same letter he states that they were to march into the desert with the Desert Column[25] on the next day having handed their boats back and had taken to the 'ships of the desert'. A last letter dated 13 January from the Gakdul Wells, written by candlelight, with his knee and a piece of wood for a table, describes his march across the desert and the scene at wells where water was the consistency of liquid mud, 'had a pretty hard time of it … four hours sleep … only 3 pints of water a day … no breakfast … and only a little biscuit … we ought to be in Khartoum in about a fortnight or less. I have in my mind's eye plenty of material for painting … four days without washing', and a brief but crucial entry in light of later events, 'got our Gardner Gun mounted and this morning drilled all our men'.

The Gardner Gun indeed proved a critical issue for the Naval Detachment as they continued the march towards the wells at Abu Klea. Lord Charles Beresford had assumed command and with the detachment was Melton Prior, the *Illustrated London News*[26] artist and correspondent, causing de Lisle momentarily to fear that he would not have any future sketches published.

On 16 January the Desert Column of 120 officers and 1,900 men[27] reached a point about six miles from the vital wells at Abu Klea and camped for the night. The enemy had kept up an incessant noise most of the night which presaged their probable intentions for the following day, 'this tom tomming is beyond all discordant noises … sound rose and swelled all night'. De Lisle found that he had no blanket and as the desert temperature could be bitterly cold even under canvas he was able to share a blanket with Lord Cochrane.[28]

The following morning at 11am the column was moving towards the wells in a military defensive square formation[29] when it was suddenly confronted[30] by a large force of the Mahdi's army. A desperate battle took place and allegedly was one of the few occasions when a British infantry square broke due to a misinterpretation of orders. Worse, however, was in store for the Naval Detachment, whose Gardner Machine Gun[31] jammed at the most desperate moment after firing

25. Wolseley now divided his force sending the Desert Column overland under the command of Maj. Gen Sir Herbert Stewart and consisting of The Heavy Camel Corps, comprising Household Cavalry, Dragoon Guards, Dragoons and Lancers. The Guards Camel Corps, comprising Grenadier, Coldstream and Scots Guards and Royal Marine Light Infantry, The Mounted Infantry Camel Corps, The Light Camel Regiment, 1st Bn Sussex Regiment and the Royal Naval detachment.
26. The ILN Paper had published seven of Rudolph's Sudan sketches prior to his death which was reported on 31 January, issue 106.
27. *Beyond the Reach of Empire* records the Nile Expedition at 115 Officers, 1687 troops, plus communication lines and native workers. The numbers of the Mahdi's forces were estimated from 5,000 to 15,000.
28. Captain the Lord Cochrane No 1 company Heavy Camel Regiment.
29. Both de Lisle and Pigott were seen by Capt W Verner of the Rifle Brigade struggling with 'recalcitrant' camels.
30. A Lieutenant Dawson stated 'as if they had risen from the earth, up rose a line of spearmen … about 5000 they came on and seemed to envelop the whole square'.
31. The Gardner mechanical machine gun was invented in 1874 and adopted by British Army. The Royal Navy had successfully tested both the Gatling Machine Gun and the Gardener but it was discovered in The Sudan that climate and dust caused the Gardner to jam with disastrous consequences.

only 85 rounds and just as their position came under sustained attack. They bore the brunt of the initial Arab tidal wave of swords and spears, resulting in two officers and six seamen being killed.

De Lisle and his colleague Lieutenant Alfred Pigott were killed quickly, their bodies found after the battle a few yards in front of the gun which had been borne back by the mass of warriors. They had both suffered extensive stab wounds but de Lisle's face was recognisable, his sword still in its scabbard although 'his pistol had been discharged which had accounted for three of his enemies'. A description of his wounds was given in a letter home to his mother by a Lieutenant Montgomerie. De Lisle's body 'was covered with more than fifty spear wounds' and 'one frightful sword cut in the chest … but his face was not so much disfigured except by blood'. Only Lord Charles Beresford survived of those manning the Gardner gun as he was pinned beneath it when it was overturned, he described de Lisle and Lt. Pigott as 'two of the most excellent officers in her Majesty's Service'.

It was a stabbing, slashing and bloody death that de Lisle suffered at Abu Klea together with Colonel Frederick Gustavus Burnaby[32] of Somerby Hall, Leicestershire, who was commanding the Royal Horse Guards and was second-in-command of the column. Although Burnaby was attempting to re-order the corner of the broken infantry square, he too fought with pistol and sword before receiving a spear thrust in the neck. He was overwhelmed and killed, together with Corporal 1076 John McIntosh[33] of the Blues, who had left the square to support him. The square quickly recovered as the Sussex and Heavy Camel Regiments 'about turned ranks' and poured a heavy fire into the 50 or so enemy who had entered the square. None of those warriors survived and their attacking Ansar colleagues eventually retreated with heavy losses. British casualties in total were 9 officers and 65 men killed, with 6 officers and 72 men wounded. Described as 'a soldier's battle: strength, determination, steadiness and unflinching courage alone could have stemmed such an onslaught',[34] it had lasted just 15 unnerving minutes.

The British dead were buried at the battle site and a memorial erected with the officers' names inscribed. There are also two large stone cairns marking graves. The memorial has survived the hot blast of the desert sand and names are still easily distinguished.

The battle marked something of a watershed for the British. Up to this time the Mahdi's warriors had been dismissed as savages but henceforward a pronounced respect was held for the courage and tenacity of the enemy troops against superior weaponry and who fought on when wounded and refused to surrender. Their lamentably grim habit of killing British troops who were giving them water or rendering first aid resulted in outrage and routinely wounded warriors were often shot dead rather than being treated or taken prisoner.[35]

---

32. Frederick Gustavus Burnaby (1842–1885) the son of the Rev. Gustavus Andrew Burnaby of Bedford and Somerby Hall Leics. Burnaby became a soldier, traveller, balloonist and writer. Somerby Hall was demolished in 1946. The poem 'Vitai Lampada' by Sir Henry Newbolt has obvious references to the battle and death of Burnaby at Abu Klea.

    The sand of the desert is sodden red,
    Red with the wreck of a square that broke;
    The Gatling's jammed and the colonel dead
    And the regiment blind with dust and smoke

33. McIntosh's Egypt and Sudan Campaign Medal with three clasps was sold in 2008 for £3,000.
34. The phrase was originally used after the Battle of Inkerman, Crimea.
35. 'Fuzzy Wuzzy' a poem written by Rudyard Kipling (1865–1936) and published in *Barrack Room Ballads* in 1892 catches the respect of the private soldier for the Mahdi's warriors: 'for all the odds agin you Fuzzy Wuz, you broke a British Square'.

De Lisle and his colleagues no doubt died bravely but to no purpose, the British Army was unable to rescue Gordon who was killed at Khartoum together with 10,000 of the Christian population when it was overrun by the Mahdi's forces during 26–27 January. Two steamers from the Nile column with less than 30 troops and Captain Charles Beresford on board managed to reach Khartoum on the 28th. With their limited resources no attempt was made to land or enter the city, the picture was clear enough, Khartoum had fallen.

Although at the time it was Gladstone who received most of the obloquy[36] for the failure to rescue Gordon, some contemporary senior army officers were also critical of Wolseley's decision to use the Nile route with all its inherent difficulties rather than an overland column march from Suakin.[37] More recent historians have also come to the conclusion that Wolseley's strategy was flawed and worse, that he attempted to hide his shortcomings and divert the blame onto others.

The Sudan was now abandoned by the British[38] until General Kitchener invaded 13 years later. From then on it was governed jointly with the Egyptians, becoming a British protectorate in 1914 and gaining independence in 1956.

There is a further memorial to Rudolph de Lisle and 12 Royal Navy personnel killed during the Sudan Campaign in the Roman Catholic church of St Elizabeth and St Henry at Sheerness, Kent, where the de Lisle Arms are displayed on the pulpit together with a brass plaque. De Lisle's engraved sword was returned to his mother by a Captain May but is no longer in the family possession. De Lisle's medal for the Egyptian Campaign 1884–5 is retained by his great nephew, Gerard de Lisle.

A great many letters were written to his grieving family by officers and men, one in particular, twelve months after the battle and containing some grisly mementoes was from Royal Navy Seaman George Williams, writing from HMS *Clyde*, Aberdeen, 25 January 1886:

> I take the liberty of writing to inform you, the enclosed letters I took from Mr. de Lisle's pockets after his sad death in the Battle of Abu Klea; also the trinkets which he had round his neck. I am sorry I could not send them sooner, as I was not sure of your address. Hoping I don't intrude or annoy in any way by doing this.[39]

The family responded with a letter, a photograph of de Lisle and a banker's order, to which Williams replied, 'I am going to spend it on having an oil painting taken from the enclosed photo of an officer I highly respected and whom I shall think often of and of the horrible scenes before my eyes on the sad day he met his death!' It is not known whether the commission was carried out.

A letter to Mrs de Lisle from Lord Charles Beresford, written at Korti on 9 March 1885, stated 'to know him was to love and respect him … I have lost a gallant, true and noble friend'.

And others from nearer home, the Co-operative Mutual Improvement Society and the Leicestershire Conservative Club both wrote to his mother expressing their profound regrets at his death.

---

36. The Liberal Government was not re-elected in 1886.
37. Suakin, a Red Sea port 480 miles northeast of Khartoum.
38. The Mahdist forces were routed at Kirkeban on 10 February 1885. Sixty British troops were killed including General Earle.
39. Family correspondence, the last three letters from his mother and scapulars made for him by his sister Gwendaline. One of these scapulars is still in the possession of the family.

Lord Tennyson had coined a phrase 'theirs not to reason why'[40] for an earlier conflict, but it no doubt resonated with the families of the Naval Detachment about how their sailor sons, water borne warriors, had incongruously met their end in an arid desert, fighting on foot, alongside camels, far from the sea.

The family homes that Rudolph de Lisle had known and lived in were eventually sold in the twentieth century, Gracedieu becoming a school and Garendon Hall being demolished in 1964. The de Lisle family later purchased Quenby Hall, Hungarton, Leicestershire, residing there until 2014.

This essay first appeared in 'Soldiers of the Queen', *The Journal of the Victorian Military Society*, issue 165, Autumn/Winter 2016, pp. 23–29.

About the Author

David Howell is a retired Police Officer, having joined the Staffordshire Constabulary in 1965. Retiring after 30 years' service he spent the next 16 years as a staff member in the same force. Married with two daughters and now four grandchildren he currently lives in Leicester. With an abiding interest in the history of British India he spends his spare time reading and writing on military history.

Sources

Archer, Thomas. *The War in Egypt and the Sudan.* 4 volumes. London: Blackie; 1885–1886.

Barthorp, M. *Blood Red Desert Sand. The British Invasions of Egypt and the Sudan 1882–1898.* London: Cassells; 2002.

Brendon, P. *Thomas Cook 150 years of popular Tourism.* London: Secker and Warburg; 1991.

Colvile, Col. H E.[41] *History of the Sudan Campaign, Parts 1 and 2.* London: War Office, Military Intelligence Department; 1899.

De Cosson, Major E.A. *Days and Nights of Service with Sir Gerald Grahams Field Force at Suakin.* Greenhill Press [reprint]; 1990.

De Lisle, Gerard, ed. *The Royal Navy and the Peruvian–Chilean War 1879–1881: Rudolph de Lisle's Diaries and Watercolours.* Barnsley: Pen and Sword Books Maritime; 2008.

Edward, Lord Gleichen. *With the Camel Corps up the Nile.* Brighton: Naval and Military Press [reprint]; 2004.

Goldston, R. *The Sword of the prophet. The Mahdi of Sudan and the Death of General Gordon.* Brighton: Naval and Military Press [reprint]; 2004.

Maclaren, R. *Canadians on the Nile.* Vancouver: University of British Columbia; 1978.

Oxenham, Rev. H. N. *Memoir of Lieut. de Lisle RN.* London: Chapman and Hall; 1887.

Royle, Charles. *The Egyptian Campaign 1882–1885.* 2 volumes. London: Hurst and Blackett; 1900.

Snook, Colonel M. *Beyond the Reach of Empire.* Frontline Books, London 2013.

Steevens, G. W. *With Kitchener to Khartoum.* London: Routledge; 1899.

Warner, P. *Dervish: The Rise and Fall of an African Empire.* New York: Taplinger; 1975.

Wilson, Sir Charles. *From Korti to Khartum.* London: Blackwoods; 1886.

40. Tennyson's poem The Charge of the Light Brigade, Crimean War 1854.
41. Colonel Herbert Edward Colvile (1852–1907) nicknamed Odger was born at Kirkby Mallory, Leicestershire and joined the Grenadier Guards in 1870. He was killed in a motorcycle accident in Surrey on 24 November 1907.

Lieutenant Rudolph M.P. de Lisle RN
(1853–1885)

Surname:	March Phillipps de Lisle	
Names:	Rudolph Edward	
Birth:	23 November 1853	
Place:	Grace Dieu Manor, Leicestershire	
Education:	Oscott College, Nr. Birmingham	Sept. 1865–June 1866
	Naval Academy, Gosport, Hampshire	Oct. 1866–Apr. 1867
	Britannia, Dartmouth	May 1867–July 1868
Service:	HMS *Victory*	July 1868–Sept. 1868
	HMS *Bristol* etc. (Gibraltar, Malta, Syracuse, Naples)	Sept. 1868–Apr. 1869
	The Flying Squadron (Rio, Vancouver, Honolulu, Australia & New Zealand, Valparaiso, Bahia (Brazil)	June 1869–Dec. 1870
	HMS *Cameleon* etc. (Callao, Lima, Tahiti, Valparaiso)	Apr. 1871–May 1875
	Naval College, Greenwich	July 1875–Apr. 1876
	Mediterranean Squadron HMS *Shannon* etc. (Montenegro, Athens, Smyrna)	May 1876–Oct. 1879 (*c.*)
	Pacific Squadron HMS *Shannon* (Peruvian–Chilean War)	Dec. 1879–June 1881
	Naval College, Greenwich	Oct. 1881–July 1882
	Mediterranean HMS *Alexandra* (Malta, Venice, Cyprus)	Jan. 1883–June 1884
	Egypt – Sudan (The Nile Expedition)	June 1884–Jan. 1885
Death:	17 January 1885	
Place:	Abu Klea Battle, Sudan	
Burial:	17 January 1885	

Place: Abu Klea Battlefield, Sudan

Decorations: Egyptian Campaign Medal (Queen Victoria)
With 2 clasps: 'Abu Klea', 'The Nile 1884–85'

Commemorations: Sheerness (R.C.) Church, Kent: Pulpit with de Lisle Coat of Arms and Plaque inscribed 'To the Catholics who fell when serving in Naval Brigade'.

Memoirs: *Memoir of Lt. Rudolph de Lisle R.N.* by the Rev. H.N. Oxenham, M.A. London. 1st Edition, March 1886, 2nd Edition, September 1886, 3rd Edition, 1887

March Phillipps de Lisle Genealogy

Who's Who

AMBROSE LISLE MARCH PHILLIPS [DE LISLE] (1809–1878)
(de Lisle added 1862 in right of his grandmother, Susan Lisle). Son of Charles March Phillipps (1779–1862) and Harriet Ducarel (1790–1813). Married 25 July 1833 Eleonora 'Laura' Mary Clifford (1811–1896). Loving father of 16 children (9 boys, 7 girls). Very early ecumenist; privately educated, then at Cambridge. Donor of land for Mt St Bernard Abbey (Cistercian). Portrait 1879. See: Canon Bernard (1911–1981) & Mrs Margaret (1922–2014) Pawley, *Faith & Family: The Life and Circle of Ambrose de Lisle*, London, 1993; E.S. Purcell (1824–1899) & Edwin de Lisle (1852–1920), *The Life and Letters of Ambrose Phillipps de Lisle*, London, 1900.

ELEONORA 'LAURA' MARY CLIFFORD, MRS AMBROSE MARCH PHILLIPPS (1811–1896)
Wife of Ambrose Lisle March Phillipps; mother of 16 children (9 boys, 7 girls); assiduous writer of 56 pertinently observed diaries. See: Alexander Cruikshank DD (1831–1900), *Laura de Lisle*, London, 1897.

AMBROSE 'AMO' CHARLES MARCH PHILLIPPS (1834–1883)
Eldest son of Ambrose and Laura March Phillipps. Married 1861 Frances Amelia Victoria Sutton (1840–1871); two sons: Everard (1862 1947) and Bernard (1864–1921). Tragically, Frances died of burns after her crinoline skirt caught fire and she was unable to free herself from her dress due to the modern metal corset stays. Ambrose remarried 1880 the Hon. Nina Violet America Sandys (*c.*1852–1905); one daughter: Gwendoline March Phillipps de Lisle, Mrs John Protheroe (1882–1962). An elusive character, Ambrose was a keen sportsman (primarily hunting and shooting).

EVERARD ALOYSIUS MARCH PHILLIPPS VC (1835–1857)
Second son of Ambrose and Laura March Phillipps. Heroic soldier who distinguished himself at the Siege of Delhi; recommended for the VC 14 September 1857, but killed by a sniper 17 September 1857, denying him the medal as they were not, at that point, given posthumously. By special permission of King Edward VII, Everard's Victoria Cross was presented to Edwin de Lisle (1852–1920), his only surviving brother, 50 years later.

REGINALD BERNARD MARCH PHILLIPPS (1839–1845)
Third son of Ambrose and Laura March Phillipps. Died after a fall; buried in Grace Dieu Chapel Crypt. Sadly, no photograph or portrait exists.

BERNARD MARY MARCH PHILLIPPS (1846–1856)
Fourth son of Ambrose and Laura March Phillipps. Died after falling on pond ice; buried in Grace Dieu Chapel Crypt.

OSMUND CHARLES MARCH PHILLIPPS (1847–1869)
Fifth son of Ambrose and Laura March Phillipps. Died of Typhoid while studying at Cirencester Agricultural College (now University). Regarded by all who knew him as an upright and pious young man.

FRANCIS 'FRANK' MARCH PHILLIPPS (1851–1883)
Sixth son of Ambrose and Laura March Phillipps. ADC to Sir Frederick Aloysius Weld GCMG (1823–1891), Governor of Western Australia. Emigrated to Western Australia, where he married 1882 Emma Thomson (1861–1899), no issue. Died suddenly of a heart attack.

EDWIN JOSEPH MARCH PHILLIPPS (1852–1920)
Seventh son of Ambrose and Laura March Phillipps. MP for Loughborough 1886–1892. Married 1889 Agnes Henriette Ida Hope (1868–1920). Eight children (5 sons, 3 daughters), his descendants are the only de Lisles left today from Ambrose and Laura's 16 children. Writer of many erudite pamphlets; a controversial figure on religious and political matters.

RUDOLPH EDWARD MARCH PHILLIPPS RN (1853–1885)
Eighth son of Ambrose and Laura March Phillipps, a brave, skilled, and capable naval officer. Died heroically at the Battle of Abu Klea, Sudan, 17 January 1885. Popular among his brother officers and a talented artist whose sketches from the Nile appeared in the *Illustrated London News*. His letters, many of which have survived, show him to be an intelligent and observant correspondent. See: Rev. H.N. Oxenham, *Memoir of Lt. Rudolph de Lisle RN*, London, 3 editions, 1886–1887; Gerard de Lisle, *The Royal Navy and the Peruvian-Chilean War 1879–1881: Rudolph de Lisle's Diaries & Watercolours*, Barnsley, 2008.

GERARD 'GERRY' LISLE MARCH PHILLIPPS (1860–1924)
Ninth and last son and last child of Ambrose and Laura March Phillipps. Educated Cirencester Agricultural College 1876–1880. Married 1902 Yvonne Louise Marie Huguette Frotier de la Coste Messelière (1869–1948); no issue. Following his divorce, emigrated to Saskatchewan, Canada, where he died, it is said, of hypothermia during a particularly bad winter.

PHILOMENA 'MENA' MARCH PHILLIPPS, LADY WELD (1836–1903)
Eldest daughter of Ambrose and Laura March Phillipps. Married 1859 Sir Frederick Aloysius Weld GCMG (1823–1891), Colonial Administrator New Zealand, Australia (Western &, later, Tasmania), Straits Settlement (Malaysia). Thirteen children (6 boys, 7 girls). 1900–1903 Mother Gertrude Delores Weld in convent St Scholastica, Fort Augustus, where her daughter, Edith (1866–1919) was Mother Superior. See: Dom Raymund Weld (1876–1952) [her son], *Life*, 1903; Prof. Noel Vose, *Mena, Daughter of Obedience*, Western Australia, 2013.

ALICE MARY MARCH PHILLIPPS, THE HON. MRS ARTHUR STRUTT (1840–1926)
Second daughter of Ambrose and Laura March Phillipps. Married 1873 The Hon. Arthur Strutt (1842–1977), 3rd son of Edward Strutt, 1st Baron Belper. Two children: Edwin Lisle Strutt (1874–1948) and Laura (1875–1909). Following

Arthur's tragic death in a factory accident, Arthur's family engaged in a long-running and bitter dispute with Alice over her son's religious education, ultimately forcing her to flee to Spain with her children and remain there for some years.

WINIFRED 'FREDA' MARY MARCH PHILLIPPS, LADY HOWARD OF GLOSSOP (1841–1909)
Third daughter of Ambrose and Laura March Phillipps. Married 1863 Lord Edward FitzAlan Howard, 1st Baron Howard of Glossop (1818–1883), his second marriage; no issue. Co-published with her brother, Gerard, *A Journal of a Tour in the US, Canada, Mexico*, London, 1897.

MARY LISLE MARCH PHILLIPPS (1843–1860)
Fourth daughter of Ambrose and Laura March Phillipps. Died, in odour of sanctity, of consumption. Buried in Grace Dieu Chapel Crypt. Only one poor quality photograph of her exists.

BERTHA MARY MARCH PHILLIPPS (1844–1913)
Fifth daughter of Ambrose and Laura March Phillipps. 1862 entered the Sisters of the Good Shepherd Order, Liverpool, as Sister Mary of St Xavier.

GWENDALINE MARY MARCH PHILLIPPS (1845–1914)
Sixth daughter of Ambrose and Laura March Phillipps. 1869 entered the Benedictine Order at Atherstone Priory (daughter house of St Benedict's Priory, Colwich) as Mother Mary Aloysia. The foundation stone of Atherstone Priory was laid by Ambrose March Phillipps in 1837.

MARGARET MARY MARCH PHILLIPPS (1855–1895)
Seventh and last daughter of Ambrose and Laura March Phillipps. Took over Ambrose March Phillipps's correspondence with Prime Minister William E. Gladstone (1809–1898). In 1886 joined The Franciscan Missionary Sisters of St Joseph (FMSJ), Third Order Regular, at the motherhouse at Mill Hill, London, founded 1883.

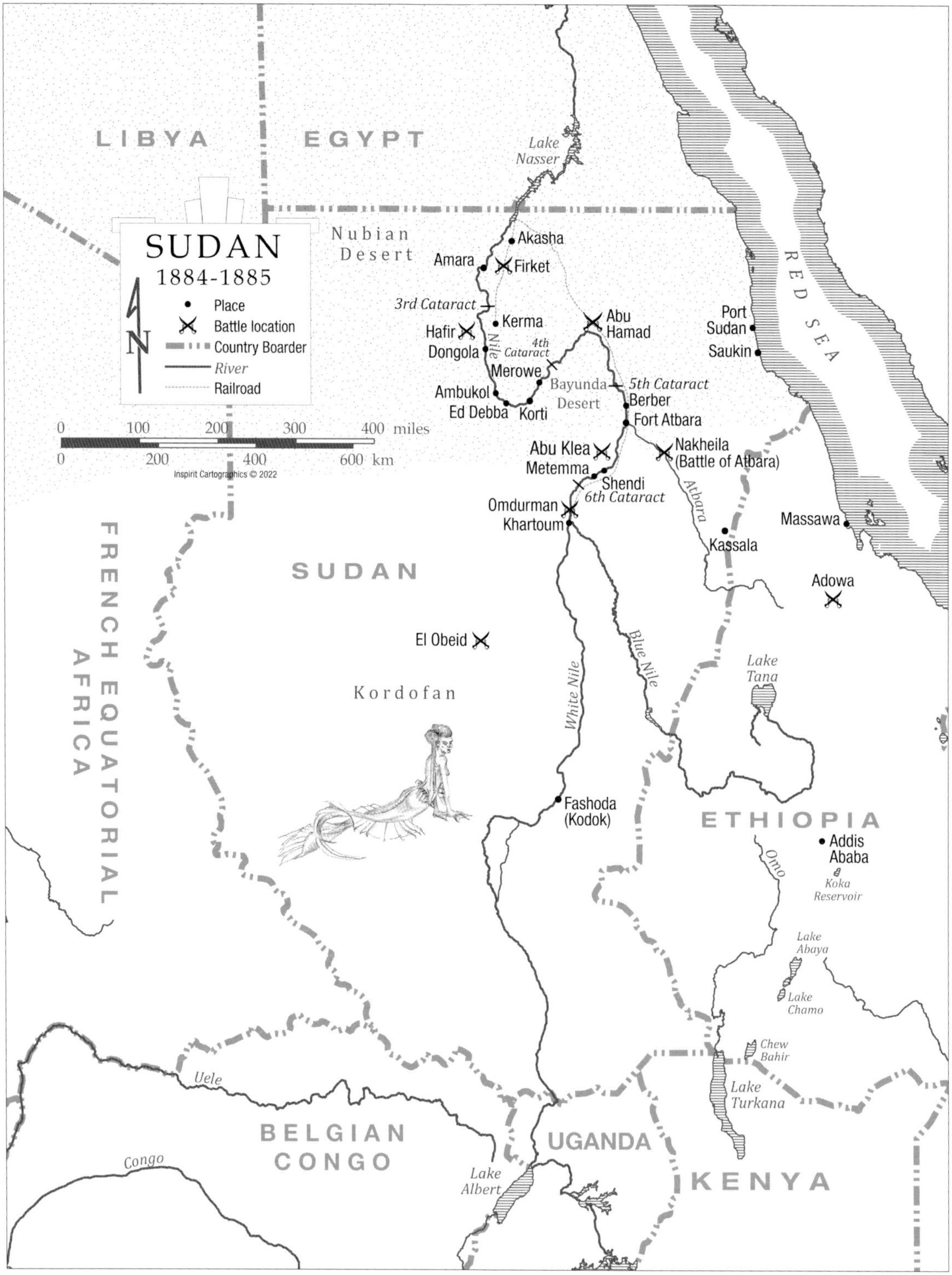
SUDAN
1884-1885
Place
Battle location
Country Boarder
River
Railroad
0 100 200 300 400 miles
0 200 400 600 km
Inspirit Cartographics © 2022
LIBYA
EGYPT
Lake Nasser
Nubian Desert
Akasha
Amara
Firket
3rd Cataract
Kerma
Abu Hamad
Hafir
Dongola
4th Cataract
Nile
Merowe
Bayunda Desert
5th Cataract
Ambukol
Berber
Ed Debba
Korti
Fort Atbara
Abu Klea
Nakheila (Battle of Atbara)
Metemma
Shendi
6th Cataract
Omdurman
Khartoum
Atbara
Kassala
Port Sudan
Saukin
RED SEA
Massawa
Adowa
SUDAN
El Obeid
Kordofan
White Nile
Blue Nile
Lake Tana
FRENCH EQUATORIAL AFRICA
Fashoda (Kodok)
ETHIOPIA
Addis Ababa
Koka Reservoir
Omo
Lake Abaya
Lake Chamo
Chew Bahir
Lake Turkana
Uele
BELGIAN CONGO
UGANDA
KENYA
Congo
Lake Albert

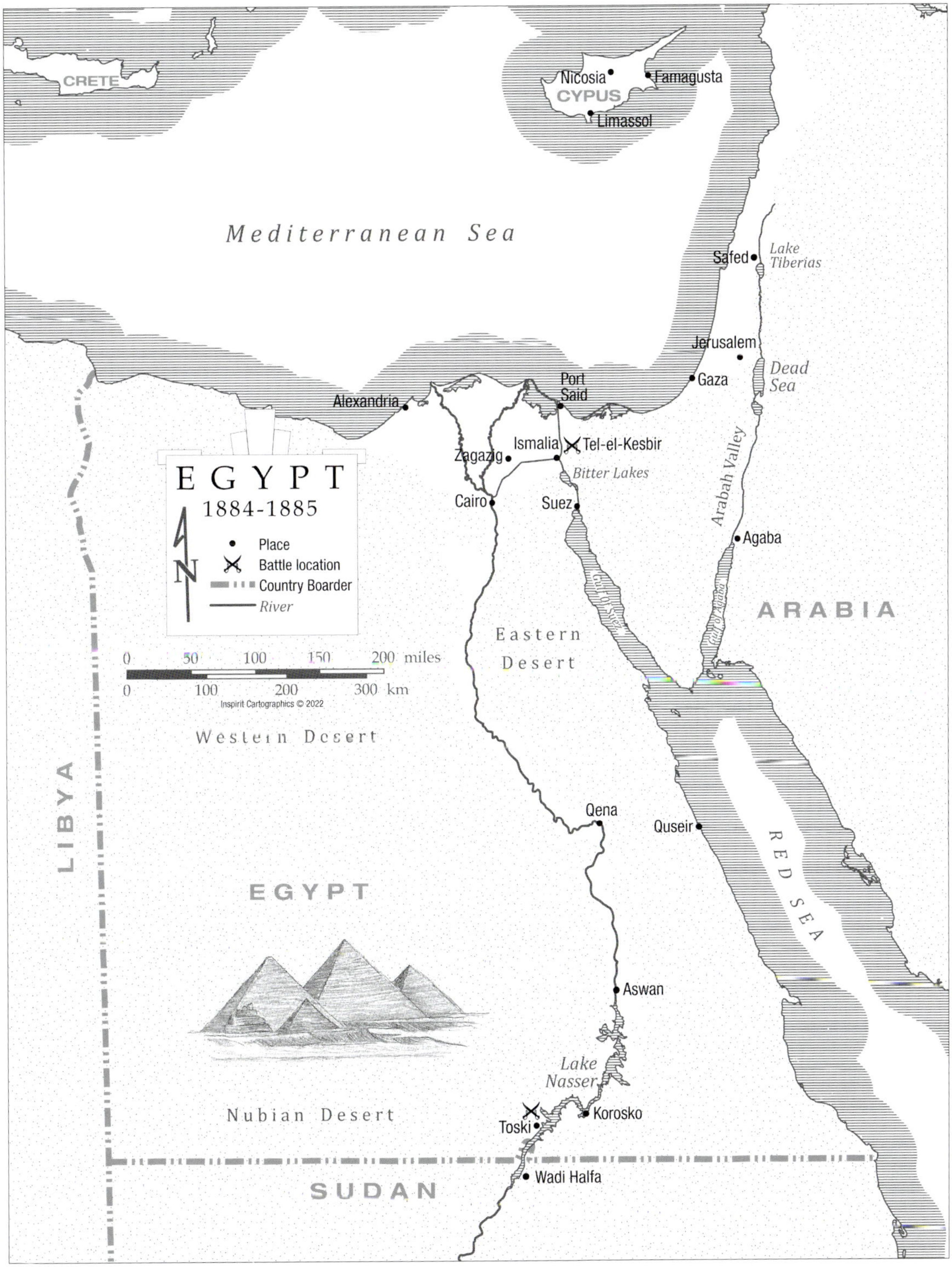
EGYPT
1884-1885
N
Place
Battle location
Country Boarder
River
0 50 100 150 200 miles
0 100 200 300 km
Inspirit Cartographics © 2022
Mediterranean Sea
CRETE
CYPUS
Nicosia
Famagusta
Limassol
Safed
Lake Tiberias
Jerusalem
Gaza
Dead Sea
Alexandria
Port Said
Ismalia
Tel-el-Kesbir
Zagazig
Bitter Lakes
Cairo
Suez
Arabah Valley
Agaba
ARABIA
Eastern Desert
Western Desert
LIBYA
Qena
Quseir
RED SEA
EGYPT
Aswan
Lake Nasser
Toski
Korosko
Nubian Desert
Wadi Halfa
SUDAN

Sketches by Rudolph de Lisle[1]

1. For a list of Rudolph's sketches submitted to the *Illustrated London News*, please see p.125.

The Letters

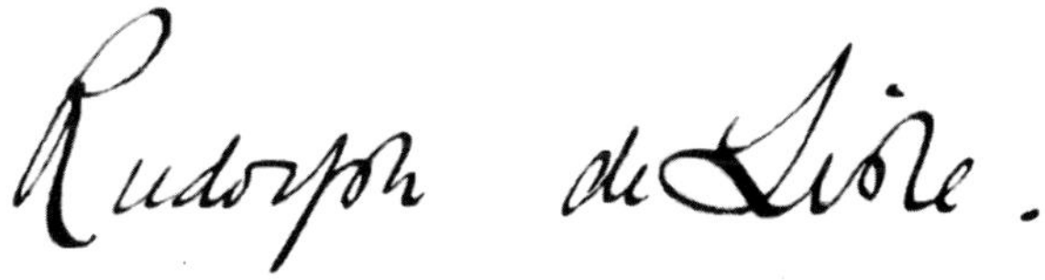

Principles of Inclusion

In 1886 the Rev. Henry Nutcombe Oxenham published *Memoir of Rudolph De Lisle, R.N. of the Royal Naval Brigade on the Upper Nile*, containing eighteen letters written by Rudolph while serving in the Naval Brigade on the Nile between August 1884 and January 1885. It was well-reviewed, immensely popular, and ran to three editions.

Oxenham was born in Harrow on 15 November 1829. Educated at Harrow and Balliol, Oxford (BA 1850, MA 1854), he took Anglican Orders in 1853, but in 1857 converted to Roman Catholicism. A regular contributor to *The Saturday Review*, he also had essays published in *Short Studies in Ecclesiastical History and Biography* and *Short Studies, Ethical and Religious*. In 1876 he translated the second volume of Bishop Hefele's *History of the Councils of the Church*, and published several pamphlets on Church Reunion, an abiding interest. The Rev. Oxenham died on 23 March 1888 at the age of 58.

In addition to Rudolph's 18 letters from The Nile, as published in the Rev. Oxenham's *Memoir*, we have chosen to include, in a separate section, five other letters; from a 7-year-old Rudolph to his mother (written in French), an 11-year-old Rudolph to his first cousin once removed, Captain (later Admiral) Alfred Ryder; two from Laura, Rudolph's mother, written to Rudolph while he was with the Naval Brigade on the Nile; and, lastly, the letter of condolence written to Laura by Lord Beresford after Rudolph's death.

We have, where possible, provided brief biographical notes for those persons making an appearance in the letters. These notes, separate to those provided by the Rev. Oxenham which appear as footnotes, can be found at the end of The Letters section. In all cases, we have retained Rudolph's occasionally unorthodox spelling, grammar and punctuation.

In the case of the letters from Laura de Lisle, suggestions for missing words or passages and those wholly indecipherable are represented within chevrons thus <   >.

Finally, we have chosen to reproduce the original language in full. Readers should be aware that Rudolph was a man of his time and, as such, on occasion he uses terms reflective of that period that are totally unacceptable today. We apologise for any offence or distress reading such language might cause.

The Nile Letters

Rudolph to his mother, Laura de Lisle

Letter 1

Rudolph to his Mother, Laura de Lisle

H.M.S. 'ALEXANDRA', OFF ALEXANDRIA,
15th August 1884

I have only time to write a few hurried lines, as I am just off up the Nile – starting from the ship at seven this evening. When I shall return again it is impossible to say, probably, from what I have heard, never again to the Alexandra, as we are going up with men, and are going to try and drag the boats (100 feet long) over the cataracts, but as the Nile is even now falling, the soldiers have declared the task impossible. The Admiral[i] informed me that sometimes what others thought impossible the navy did not, and therefore we were selected to go and try. One thing is sure; I have now got the *task*, up the Nile, if not the trip of patrolling the river, which is much easier work. And after we have finished I hope, if General Dormer[ii] has command of the force, to get our company pushed on to the front.

Up the Nile the weather, I hear, is somewhat warm, but I trust we shall come well out of it all, and if there is a chance I hope we may take it, but of one thing *you* may be certain; we shall do our *best* in every way. We are starting on a good day, 15th August, so I trust everything may be successful. … I have capital officers with me; Pollen[iii] is in my company, I am glad to say, and a great friend of mine; Commander Hammill[iv] is the man I have to thank, for I hear he applied for me when he heard the work the navy had to do. All I hope is to be spared health and strength not to sell him and the navy generally in this matter. I shall write as soon as possible, but most probably only a few lines at a time.

Good-bye, my dearest mother. For all our sakes do take the greatest care of yourself.

Stone Dam and Water Collection, 18 August 1884.

Letter 2

Rudolph to his Mother, Laura de Lisle

S.S. 'BENHAH', OFF KENEH,
19th August 1884

I am writing this letter on the chance of sending it to-day from here, where we remain for the night, and to-morrow morning start off again for Assouan, where we ought to arrive Thursday or Friday next. We then move on with all despatch to Wady Halfa, then on to the cataracts. And, now that the plan of proceeding is divulged, owing to the dilatoriness of the Government making up their minds a month too late, I doubt whether it is possible to get eight steamers over eighteen cataracts in less than month from now, for the distance they have to be assisted is 230 miles, and this without roads and only short provisions, every pound of which has to be carried, and the steamers loaded and unloaded at the cataracts. However, we shall do our utmost, and our leader, Commander Hammill, has the reputation of being a very good man. Still I don't believe much in his method, but we shall more or less be able to use our own methods. But it is just this: after dragging these boats over the cataracts by the smallest mistake all our exertions may be lost in a moment, and there is no doubt getting the towing hawsers through the rapids will cause loss of life, and perhaps more than is thought. There is, I fear, if successful, no possibility of getting beyond Dongola, and then there is a march over the desert of 170 miles. This, unless the Bishereens, who are the great camel tribe, are friendly, will be more or less impossible, but it is confidently expected they will give every possible assistance for backsheesh; they nearly all will do anything for it.

I hope the Government now know what they intend to have done, for otherwise it is not worth while giving us all a chance of sunstroke for nothing. I am sorry to say one of our best men was knocked down yesterday, after the work of transporting our baggage in the sun, but I now trust he will pull through. I have been keeping him with wet bandages and in the shade ever since. We have a doctor on board the Alexandra, May;[i] but of course he can only order certain steps to be taken.

We received a wonderful ovation on leaving the Cairo barracks and had the band and pipers ahead of us during our march, three miles, to the station. We had expected to have remained there the night at least, but we were ordered off with all despatch, and we were glad to be getting to the scene of our work. This part of the Nile is hot; three soldiers were killed outright the day before yesterday, but they drink a lot of beer and then go out in the sun. I may be rashly judging the 46th,[ii] for these men may have been teetotallers, but I am judging by barrack life generally.

We arrived in Cairo at 10 a.m. instead of 5, marched to barracks, had breakfast, provided by the 42nd Highlanders[iii] – and most civil they were – and drew our campaigning stores, for though we have to look out to feed ourselves, the commissariat provide the stores, and we have to arrange to carry it. We are taking mountain tents with us, &c., &c. Train left at 7.30 p.m., the General (Nicholson)[iv] coming to see us off; Captain Hammill (our Commander) kindly introduced

On the way to Keneh. Sketched on 19 August on the way to join the SS *Benhah* to travel up the Nile, 19 August 1884.

Three sketches made while travelling on the SS *Benhah*, 18/19 August 1884.

20

Helmsman at the Wheel.
Inset: Our Pilot.

me to him just as we were leaving. We got to Assouan at 10 next morning (17th August 1884) and got everything on board this craft, then organized our arrangements, &c. on board, for we are still a perfectly organized small ship's company, consisting in all of seventy-three men and officers, and our direction now is, *Naval Brigade, Wady Halfa, or above.* There is absolutely no moisture in the air, and one's ink dries as fast as one writes, and for this reason the weather is not at all unbearable. I have had a lot of work to do already in the sun and, thank God, I haven't felt the sun as yet, and if the weather was damp it would be perfectly unbearable. At Suakin in the Red Sea the marines are burying a man a day from sunstroke. … Do not be afraid if you do not hear for a long time from me after we pass Wady Halfa, for there may or may not be any opportunity of sending letters, and we have rough times before us, but at last I am on the spot, and let us hope something will turn up this time. … Already two more lieutenants have been appointed to the Alexandra, so I expect I have finished with her. …

P.S. If only there can be a chance of securing what Everard[v] failed actually to secure,[1] how happy I should be, but I fear our work is only helping soldiers over the Falls, and there we shall remain. But who knows?

1. Oxenham – The Victoria Cross. Everard, Rudolph's elder brother, whose name has frequently occurred in the course of this narrative, joined the Native Infantry of the Bengal Presidency in 1854. He reached Meerut on 4 May 1857, and on May 10, when the mutiny broke out, his regiment joined it, and Colonel Finnis was killed at his side; but he remained unhurt, though he had been called upon to read the address in Hindustani. On the same day he joined the 60th Rifles, when he obtained a commission on the application of Colonel Jones, who made him his orderly officer. The following memorandum appeared in the *London Gazette* of 21 October 1859, p.3793: 'Ensign Everard Aloysius Lisle Phillipps, of the 11th Regiment, Bengal Native Infantry, would have been recommended to Her Majesty for the decoration of the Victoria Cross, had he survived, for the many gallant deeds which he performed during the siege of Delhi, during which he was wounded three times. At the assault of that city, he captured the Water Bastion, with a small party of men and was finally killed in the streets of Delhi on the 17th of September.'

Letter 3

Rudolph to his Mother, Laura de Lisle

P.S. 'GHIZEH' NEAR WADY HALFA, UPPER NILE,
25th August 1884

We are now at last approaching our destination, and from here we disembark and go by train only four or five miles up towards the second cataract, which is our base of operations. There we shall have our camp, and by degrees get our stores ready to attempt hauling the vessels over the cataract. We are to have, if they all turn up, from 3,000 to 5,000 niggers, Arabs, &c., to do the manual work, but of our work more when it begins, and when we know what it is we have before us. The Nile has fallen already four feet, but the natives seem to think it will rise again in another three weeks' time. The later the Nile is the better our chance of success. All along the river we continually meet diebhrs, or house-boats, full of stores, coal, &c., but owing to contrary winds and the strong tide they are in the same position nearly they were in a week ago, viz., off Korosko. I think I cannot do better than give you a short account from my journal, a few lines each day.

August 15*th*. – Landed at Alexandria and went to Cairo with our party, consisting of Commander Hammill, Lieutenants Pigott[i] and de Lisle, Sub-Lieutenant Pollen, and two engineers and seventy-one men. … I find I have been repeating so I omit everything to Luxor.

August 20*th*. – Ruins of Luxor and Carnac are splendid in their way, but we hurried through, so that of course we could only get a general view without being able to see any of the hieroglyphics or inscriptions except the ones of the pillars, which are clearly discernible even at a distance. I made a few sketches, but Carnac and Luxor are places where one could spend days sketching, and a column reproduced on an intelligible scale would take a few hours' work of itself, so you can imagine the magnitude of the attempt to do the whole thing as the ships steamed by. At Luxor, which is a charming place, groves of palms and other trees, splendid ruins, a decent hotel, a Catholic church, numerous diebhrs (house-boats), &c., some on their way up, others with their large sails down for drifting down with the stream. In the afternoon passed the Tombs of the Kings, and the two colossal figures of Rameses II (sixty feet high), on the left bank. Arrived at Esneh, met Major Stuart-Wortley[ii] and party; they were nearly lost in the desert, got off the track, but in sixteen hours fortunately found it again; otherwise they would not again have been heard of. Got news that Major Kitchener[iii] was returning from his expedition across the desert to Khartoum.

August 21*st*. – Passed some ancient ruins, Tombs of the Kings, 8.30. Arrived off Kosmombo, but being pitch dark, as we were close to the ancient temple, we landed with lanterns and spent a couple of hours looking at the ruins. The inscriptions were in many cases quite perfect, and the paintings as perfect as if put on only a few years. It shows what a wonderfully dry climate it is. We have had the temperature from 95° to 103° under awnings, and found the weather not at all unpleasant, whereas at Port Said with the glass at 82° it was almost unbearable.

Collage of three sketches showing: the Ruins of Carnac; another view of the Ruins of Carnac; a Coptic Convent.

Temple of Abu Simmel/Simbel – two views, 25 August 1884.

Temple of Philae and Nile Scene.

Preliminary pencil sketch of Sheik Basheir.

Later watercolour of Sheik Basheir.

Sheik Basheir's entourage following him along the bank.

Sheik Basheir's men waiting for him on the bank.

Korosko, 24 August 1884.

August 22nd.—Arrived at Assouan at 9.30, and had to make arrangements for a train to take us over to Philæ, where also there are splendid ruins of temples, &c. We turned over to the train and started at 2.30 for Philæ, having finished the first part of the picnic, and turned over to the Ghizeh, one of the vessels commanded by naval officers—viz., Reed,[iv] and a great friend of mine—for the trip to Halfa. One of our men unfortunately misbehaved, broke into our wine store, and had to be sent to a vessel to await passage to the Alexandra. One man went down with the sun, but since recovered.

August 23rd, 5 a.m.—Passed two companies of the 35th Regiment[v] on their way to Halfa. 2 p.m., stopped and took on board Sheik Basheir, a splendid fellow, very handsome and, like all Arabs, most dignified. He is friendly, and chief of the tribe of Bishareens, which counts 17,000 men, stretching right across to the Red Sea. They are all mounted on camels, or rather dromedaries, and his was a beautiful creature and snow white. He came on with us as far as Korosko, where he was given a splendid reception by his men, who gave a war-dance on the banks, and a most interesting performance it was. I landed in the evening and made a sketch of his party, who had followed on by the banks.

August 24th.—Arrived off Korosko about 4 p.m. Landed and saw the fort made by Egyptians under English officers. How hot they must have made themselves over it, digging a ditch eleven feet wide and fourteen feet deep all round it; but I think there isn't the smallest possible chance of the Mahdi's[vi] followers ever attempting an attack on the place, for

Major Shakespeare's tent.

Officer sketching. Undated; probably a self-portrait.

though it is the caravan route, it is three days and a-half from the nearest wells at Abou Hamad, so neither men nor camels would be at all fit for work after marching across the desert, and likely enough the troops will be moved along. Major Shakespeare[vii] showed me over the fort, and his hut was a picture. He pitched it in the most picturesque place, with a huge cactus kind of plant at the door, and from the inside one imagines one's self in a ball-room, without the ladies however. I wish our tents were like theirs, which are tall and roomy, which means coolness, but ours are mountain ones and consequently very low; we can just get inside (room for two) stooping. These other ones are, perhaps, in the centre thirteen feet high, any amount of ventilation. We tried to get Indian tents in Cairo, but failed owing to their scarcity. Before we left we were visited by the English officers of the garrison (600 strong) and our friendly sheik left us. I did two small water-colours of him, and he wanted them; so I then did two for myself. He was exceedingly pleased with the attention showed him, but he took a special fancy to Pollen's pipe, so it had to be given to him. He wanted my tobacco, which was very little, but this I could not quite see, so I filled his pipe as often as he wished whilst on board, but to take the whole lot I couldn't and didn't quite agree to, however much my admiration for him.

It is astonishing the amount of ruins there are. Only to-day we passed a fortified Roman town, which looks as old as some of the Egyptian monuments, but of course it is not; but the astonishing part of it is that no end of the inscriptions were covered with stucco by the early Christians, and thus preserved in the marvellous way they are. There are here and there Copt villages, and in the part of Egypt below Keneh there are a great many Coptic Christians, about one-third I was told. There is one monastery we passed which I sketched, where a very curious custom prevailed. As soon as a diebhr appeared coming up stream, out sprang the monks, stripped, and swam off to the vessel – for backsheesh for their

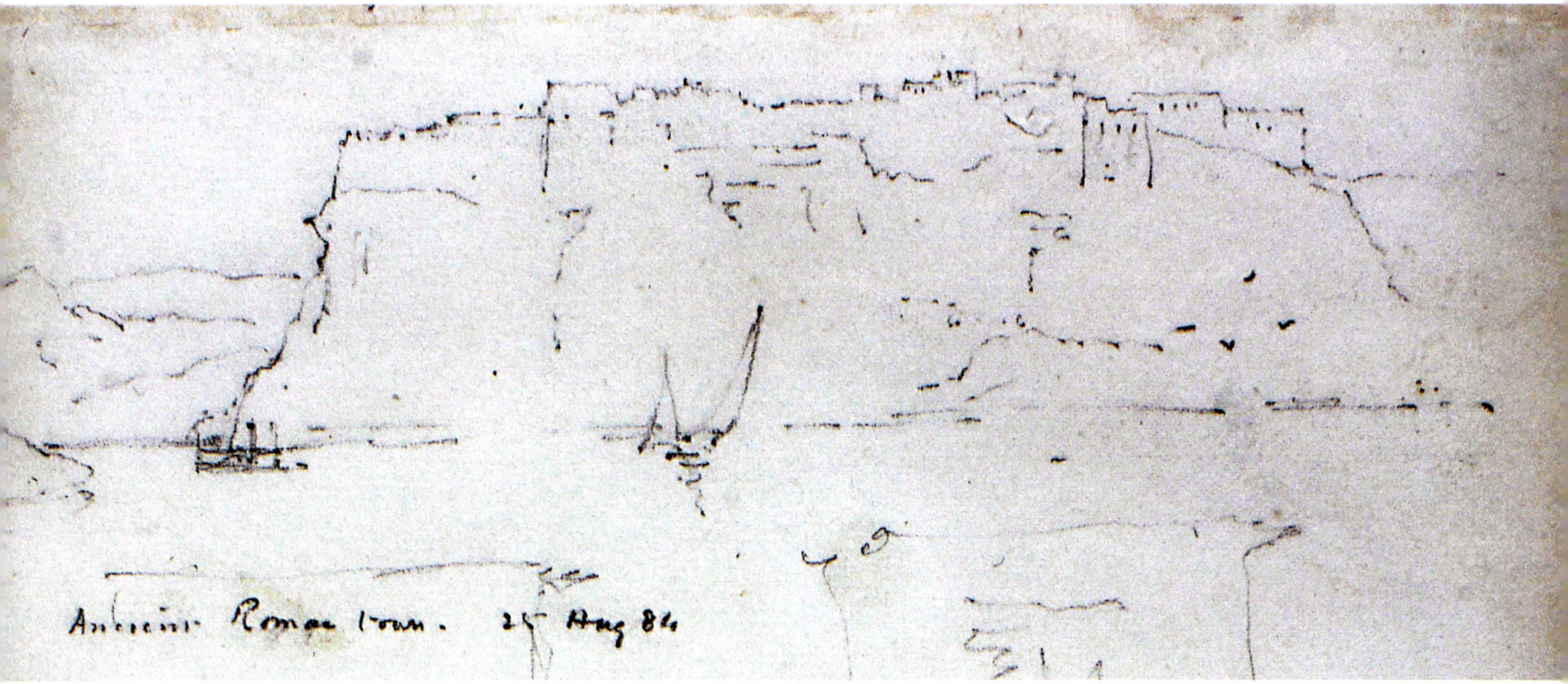

Ancient Roman Town, 25 August 1884.

monastery, I suppose! This custom has now been stopped by the Patriarch at Cairo, and just as well I should think. Round Korosko and for many miles on the left bank is all sand, of a peculiar red-yellow colour, with here and their clumps of date-palms, whilst on the other side are barren hills, brown and purple in colour, masses of red and black granite – the former very much like Aberdeen – and a thin strip of land cultivated and lines of palms, small villages dotted about, whilst the sakiehs worked by oxen in this part irrigate the land close to the bank, which yields no less than three crops per year; but further on, 300 or 400 yards inland, owing to the difficulty of supply, it yields only one crop a year, for there is never any rain – but what exquisite tints morning and evening anything more beautiful there could not be; and I simply smoke or take and take or rather devour them. Unfortunately at the last moment I had to pack up, as we expected to leave at 8p.m., and left instead at 4. So many colours were left behind and much useless gear brought, which I shall leave behind here.

A Sak-Riale half-way between Ambigol and Semneh. Rudolph later submitted a smaller version of this sketch to the *Illustrated London News* as part of a collage of six sketches showing the wreck of SS *Ghizeh*. The *Illustrated London News* used the other five sketches on their front cover of 6 December 1884 but omitted this one.

Letter 4

Rudolph to his Mother, Laura de Lisle

CAMP OF THE NAVAL BRIGADE, ABKAR,
September 8th, 1884.

Since I last wrote we have been shifting about, camp and all, first with a party of men in one place and then in another; and I regret to say the Nile has been falling ever since, and now it is no less than two feet lower than it was, the result being that the chances are infinitely small of hauling the steamers over.

On the 3rd we started off in the 'Nassif Khier', and, after eight hours of the hardest work, succeeded in getting her over what is called the First Gate of the cataract, about three miles by water from our camp, and there she has remained ever since. Commander Hammill made up his mind the Nile was going to rise again, and so we waited in the vain hope, and now we shall have to make the best of the low Nile. After surveying the best route we came to the conclusion that the outer one was the best, and now for some reason or other, with less water, we are going to try the other. I went down with six blue-jackets, right down over the third and lower gate, and I came to the conclusion that, even with the men we have (nearly 4,000 Dongolese and Esneh men) it is impossible, without smashing up the paddles, to get her through the narrow gate. The difficulties are endless, such as getting the men from one island to another, for the current rushes over ridges of rocks in a foaming torrent, and the Esneh men won't think of facing the water. About 200 of the others are magnificent swimmers and go in, in the boldest way, and are a good deal of use driving through some of the parts; but, as you may imagine, it is one thing to get over them and another to work the hawsers satisfactorily to be of real use. We are going to make another attempt to-morrow, and with what success I will report in my next letter; but as there are two correspondents you will probably by to-morrow evening know all about it. The idea of getting the other steamers over is abandoned owing to the Nile falling, but it is most provoking that this year it should have started going down ten or twelve days before the usual time, but there it is; and I fear we shall have nothing to do if we fail to get the 'Nassif Kheir' over, and in that case this trip will not have turned up trumps; – but who can tell?

One thing I do know is, we are soon likely to go bare-footed, for already I've destroyed two pairs of boots: leather perishes at once, unless they get soaked in oil, and that one hasn't got in any quantity, and during the day the rocks, which are of black granite of syenite, and the sand get so hot you can't touch them. The result is that the nails drop out of one's boots, the stitches crumble away, and off come the soles! but fortunately I brought two more pairs with me. The heat, as registered by thermometer, is very great – went up to 110° under double tents – but the heat is dry, and beyond parching one's throat and boots, which are much more important, one gets on very well. We have had a few cases of sunstroke, but fortunately no really bad ones, and personally I have only had a few hours under the tents in the middle of the day for two or three days since being out here. I ride camels all over the place, and the pleasure of riding an Arab pony after it! Colonel Trotter,[i] a friend of mine at Angush (Wady Halfa), lent me his one day to ride out to camp, and the difference was something marvellous. One jolts, when one is trotting fast, one's very soul out of one, and other was like an arm-

Naval Brigade Camp, Abkar, 30 August 1884.

Dongola men swimming across cataract. Rudolph's original sketch and how it appeared in the *Illustrated London News*, 4 October 1884.

Rock climbing.

chair. When the camels are doing their jog-trot six miles an hour it is pleasant enough, but everything depends on a comfortable saddle and a good trotting animal. Everything dries so fast that, even if one had time, there is very little use in trying to paint, and especially a place like this, where the skies are all one tint: for week after week one never sees the shadow of a cloud, and as long as the sun remains up one is broiled. I always find about 9 a.m. the most trying time of all. We heard a great deal about crocodiles up here, but I have not seen any, though others declare they saw two. Anyhow, we bathe (the officers up here), though we will not let the men risk it, and though the water is as dirty as the very worst ditch-water, it is sweet and good. I drink simply buckets full of it, and at one time expected all sorts of direful calamities owing to it, but it must be all right, for the natives drink it all day long. But to give you an idea of the amount of mud there is in it, in the whole of the irrigation work it is owing to the water evaporating and the residue of mud left, which really raises such fine crops of maize all down the river banks, for underneath it is all sand up here. There are not even any date-palm trees, and no shelter of any sort or description, but out in the sun one doesn't want it.

The first thing I did – as we all did pretty well – was to get the whole of my hair cut off as close as scissors would take, and now it stands straight on end like a scrubbing-brush, and regularly dried up. I got dear Alice's letter a few days ago – the only news I have had for a long time. … By the bye, a few days ago we were carting niggers across the river, and we got shot down one of the rapids, and it is astonishing how invariably a back wash got one clear of the rocks: exceedingly exciting it was. Yesterday we spanned the river with a hawser with block on. It was one of the worst places, and now we can run niggers across without the danger of the hawser snapping. The 35th sailed yesterday in boats, when we ought with luck to have been with them to tow them along to Dongola.

Colonel Trotter, 27 August 1884.

Letter 5

Rudolph to his Mother, Laura de Lisle

NAVAL CAMP, ABKAR, NUBIA, 2ND CATARACT,
September 18th, 1884.

At last I have a little time to write to you, the first time for a fortnight, for even when our men have been having an hour or two to spare we have been surveying the best places for securing necessary ropes for hauling steamers over. During the last fortnight it has been a case of work from twelve to fourteen hours a day, and the last few days ten miles through loose sand added on. But with the exception of two or three men with dysentery we are all right, and not sorry to-day to have a day in camp, as, thank God! we have at last got the steamer, 'Nassif Kheir', over the cataract. The river during the time fell seven feet at the worst place, Bab-el-Kebir, and the width varied from thirty-eight feet to half a mile; innumerable islands, more rocks, shoals, etc., swift-running currents, and worse eddies. But here we are; some of us have had more escapes than one, and the whole affair is not devoid of danger. Going through one of the easy bits a boat swamped, and three men were unfortunately drowned. Within two days their bodies were found by swimmers, 300 of whom were on the look-out, and all were buried outside our camp – a very mournful scene – in the same grave and together, as they were drowned; three volleys over the grave, and all over. The curious part of it was that a man belonging to the Monarch, Commander Hammill's coxswain (the man who steered his boat), Woodcock[i] by name, floated up close to the Commander's tent, about a mile from the place of the accident. One man was drowned (Hares[ii]) trying to save the others, and two more were nearly done for, but we were lucky not to have lost two boats' crews, for we were shot down the cataract. The ship herself ran tremendous risk at times, but, thank God, she is all right now. The task seemed well-nigh impossible, but it has proved possible.

Sand and dust, winds and flies, are the worst things we have to put with, but nothing can stand the heat. The rocks and sand during the day become so hot one can hardly stand on them, and already two pairs of my boots have succumbed, and a third I give another week or so over the sharp granite rocks. The bone of my knife broke and crumbled away, and everything perishes in the heat. The nights are, however, cool, which is a great comfort, for were the nights like the day nobody could stand it for long. But for the honour of the Navy I am glad to say we got our steamer over. A short time ago I got a charming letter from Alice[iii] [Mrs. Strutt] which gave me the news of Cecily's[iv] engagement, and a day or two later one from Lady Clifford,[v] and these are all I have had since up here; but with the ship moving about and no regular transport, one can only get one's letters by chance with any speed, though sooner or later they are sure to turn up, and thoroughly acceptable they will be. Three Sundays running we have been working all day and never a moment to one's self, but now we may have easier times on Sundays unless we go to the front.

I am rather amused to see in the papers about the disturbed state beyond Wady Halfa. I have been thirty miles south of it nearly, with nothing but a stick, and never met with anything except profound respect from the natives, and yet the papers talk about the armed train, etc., and patrols along the Nile as far as Dongola. Everything is quiet and now the 35th are gone on the moral effect will be very great on the natives, for the Mudir thinks his men, about 200 Circassians

The steamer *Nassif Kheir* passing the first gate of the second cataract, *Illustrated London News*, 4 October 1884. (Rudolph's original sketch lost.)

The *Nassif Kheir* passing up the Bab-el-Kebir, 16 September 1884. Published *Illustrated London News*, 25 October 1884. See overleaf.

THE NACSIF-KHEIR PASSING UP THE BAB-EL-KEBIR, THE "GREAT GATE" OF THE SECOND CATARACT.

THE NILE EXPEDITION: SKETCHES BY AN OFFICER.

and Turks, a formidable array, and with these even he kept more or less order; once the troops are there everything will be more or less quiet. Though we are so far to the front, we really know little or nothing of what is really going on, and whether we are going to have the Soudan under our wing or not. 3 p.m. – Just heard that in all probability we are going to form part of the Naval Brigade,[vi] so we must be on the lookout for better times. We are to try to take another steamer over, but the wear and tear of having to drive 3,000 niggers, who hardly understand one, is tremendous, and it has turned me white! 'Thirty large cargo boats, etc., etc.' – this is Lord Wolseley's[vii] telegram. To-morrow, I suppose, we shall begin the whole affair over again with the experience gained by the first steamer's passage over. I can hardly write, so maddened am I by the flies, dozens settling on my raw nose and lips, but by degrees one gets accustomed to these torments, and, thank goodness, there are no mosquitoes. The food we get is very good, and enough, but later on we shall be away from all luxuries in camp. Here we have a cook and a servant, and so are well off, as long as we can make the most of what we have in the way of comfort. In a blanket under a tent one sleeps very comfortably indeed, but I shall be delighted when the real business begins, moving on with the troops.

How are all the family getting on? I trust Margaret[viii] is well. She must write, for cut off up here a letter of any sort is a great boon. I hope Gerard's[ix] crops have done well this year, and he is as happy as may be. … I know what grief, my dearest mother, this day or rather anniversary brings to you.[1] If only one day I could get the Cross you should then have had; but there is infinitely more peril on the flood than in the field out here. But I trust and pray we may meet when this is over, for I don't expect to rejoin the Alexandra again, I fear. I intend to write to Lord John[x] shortly; he has been most civil to me, and I have a chance which most naval officers would like to have. You must pray it may turn up trumps.

With love to all, and ask Gerard to look out for my affairs.

It will be seen from the following extract from a letter of the same date as the last, addressed to Lady Clifford, that Rudolph had himself incurred far more serious personal risk than – with his habitual thoughtfulness for others—he cared to let his mother know.

Who can tell what will be the end of this business up here? Do not let my mother know, but I am singularly fortunate to be writing this letter now, for twice with my boat I was swept over the cataract getting hawsers (large ropes) down to the steamer when she was in danger of smashing up; and the second time my boat dashed over the rocks and water flowed over her, but fortunately I got the end of rope to steamer, and saved the men, two very nearly gone. Two days after, in an easier place the boat swamped, and this time three men were drowned, and we nearly lost two more, one insensible when got in. The whole of this expedition out here has been and is full of dangers to life and limb. The heat in the day tremendous, but fortunately perfectly dry: … the Nile instead of rising has been steadily falling, and is now seven feet lower than it was a fortnight ago. The same way I take it impossible to get another steamer over without knocking holes through her, but we shall see what can be done. We have now been under tents over a month, and the nights are now cool, which is a great blessing. Had the Government made up their minds a month or five weeks sooner, I believe we should have got two or three steamers over by this time. To give you an idea of the work in hand, in addition to our 80 men all told, we have nearly 3,000 niggers of all sorts – Dongola and Esneh men; the steamer is now in the former whilst we are in Nubia. Since up here I have never seen a crocodile, but the natives say there are always some about, and one was shot opposite our camp whilst the steamer was lying here.

1. His brother Everard was killed at Delhi, on 17 September 1857, as has already been mentioned.

Letter 6

Rudolph to his Mother, Laura de Lisle

NAVAL CAMP, ABKAR, NUBIA,
September 26th, 1884.

Since I last wrote to you I received your two most welcome letters of the 25th August and September 3rd, so I am now thankful to have such late news from home.

The first steamer we got over the cataract went all right as far as Sarras, and then struck on a rock two miles from that place, and is at present repairing, but expects to get on to Semneh to-day or to-morrow. We have had another steamer, the 'Ghizeh', to take up. Till yesterday the Nile has been steadily falling, and we had to find a new passage at the Second Gate to get the steamer through, there being no water in the passage of the rapid where the 'Nassif Kheir' passed through. We all but got through it after four days' hard work, but the difficulties of laying out the hawsers over such long sweeps of rapids, and the rottenness of the hawsers sent to us [was such] that we were doomed to failure; but on the fourth day (yesterday) we got her over, and at present she is in here at the camp. It seemed at one time as if she was never coming any further without being wrecked on the rocks. You never saw such a place; nothing but rocks, rapids, and eddy currents, which swing the ship about anyhow. To-day the steamer is repairing, and to-morrow moves on again. At Bab-el-Kebir the ship had to be dragged up-hill over a sheet of water with high rocks on both sides, but this vessel will have to go by another channel, as the sheik says there is no water; but I trust the Nile may rise a few more inches, and then it is possible. Montgomerie[i] in a fast 'picket' boat is up here, but then she steams thirteen knots and tears over the bad places remarkably well. He expects to be at Sarras to-day. Another launch has been sent up by train.

Pollen was nearly killed by a hawser (rope) yesterday, but got off with a few bruises. The friction lit up a box of matches in his trousers pocket, and he was somewhat burnt. As the squeeze came, a nigger got between him and the rock, and so that poor wretch got the phizzing box of matches against his bare skin and couldn't move. We have thin ropes from rock to rock over rapids to get at the ships, and look out for the ropes to drag her and make her fast: a few touches with a pen will give you a sort of idea. … I find being accustomed to athletics comes in most usefully, for at first the tars were somewhat shy of the *bridges*. Last Sunday knocked a plank out of our only boat and she was rapidly filling, but got her ashore just in time. Got to steamer by ropes and had a couple of hours carpentering, and she has worked fairly well ever since; tin-lined the boat inside and out near damaged part. The blue-jackets[ii] were somewhat amused when one turned up with a bag of tools and all necessaries, after an hour's absence, and somewhat pleased when the boat was repaired, for we were all cut off from mainland. There was only one carpenter on board the steamer, and he could not get over by rope bridges. We are out at 5, and sometimes get back by 7 p.m., often without anything to eat during daylight, for, though we take food with us, when it comes to time to eat work of anxious kind is going on, and likely enough lunch is cut off by a cataract – but we generally make up for it when we return to camp. The next few days will be harder work still, but

Final and successful attempt to get the steamer over the Second Gate of the cataract, 25 September 1884. Rudolph's original sketch for image 1 of the *Illustrated London News* front cover, 1 November 1884. See page 69.

Appliances for getting hawsers over the river at the second cataract. Published in the *Illustrated London News*, 4 October 1884. Rudolph's original sketch has been lost.

About 4 miles from Ambigol looking towards hills of Dal, 5 November 1884.

the climax comes always at the main gate. I often think how everything one learns comes in, and by your giving us when children our boxes of tools I learnt a lot of carpentering, and that has come in most useful; sewing also, for the desire of seeing one's self look somewhat clean has been detrimental to one's clothes, and I find myself when there are a few minutes to spare patching them. Fortunately, another pair of boots has turned up from the ship for me, and that is the chief thing, for the heat burns everything through. I am afraid you must think me terribly egotistical, but as you always like to know what one is doing, I purposely write a good deal which might be omitted.

When we left the ship, Pigott was in command of the party and I was second, but since then Hammill (Com.) has been the head, and now they have appointed a captain; so one finds one's self going down the list; but we all have separate duties to perform, so there is no clash, and I have charge of the camp and company when they fall in, and *not* as a working or cataract party. I see they have made appointments of lieutenants to the Alexandra, and I suppose we have all finished with that ship. I confess I am sorry for it, in case this is a shorter affair than one expected, and as for one's thinking for one moment of being promoted out of it, it is outside the possible chances, unless one gets into action. One thing is I never knew what work was till up here, and I regret to say our sailors frequently see officers doing what they ought to risk doing themselves. I regret to say it has been noticed by military men who have been with us. That accident we had has had curiously enough a disastrous effect upon them, and together with the rotten boat we have to work in they hate the water and work too, if the truth was known, but no doubt it will wear off in time. In the meanwhile it is the most cold-blooded work one could have, and every day might see the last of one; but of course one knew that to do what the authorities called an impossible task could not be done without risk. I wish we were at the front, for two regiments have now passed us, and I feel sure no glory will be got out of the cataract work, and the wear and tear is enormous. ....

Our only hope is you may be spared to all of us for many, many years to come.

Letter 7

Rudolph to his Mother, Laura de Lisle

NAVAL CAMP, ABKAR, NUBIA,
October 22nd, 1884.

[1]I am quite shocked to think how long it is since I have written to you, but, even had I had time, till to-day I should have been unable to do so, having knocked a finger out of joint; but it is going on all right, as this letter shows. Our life and existence up here has been of late monotony itself, hauling nuggars (native sailing boats) over the cataract – always the same old thing, and nothing to vary the work. A regular slave drive now it is to get these natives to do any work at all, and they are heartily sick of it. They are, of course 'volunteers' (?), and have soldiers to look after their interests and prevent them bolting off to Dongola, but no end of men have deserted in spite of every precaution. The 'Ghizeh', I am glad to say, is over Semneh Cataract at last. The Egyptian soldiers just made the difference, and she went over flying. At Semneh there are really only two gates, one bad, but the difficulty with the last was, owing to the abruptness of the shore, to get the hawsers placed properly. Anyhow, I trust she is on her way to Dongola now. We have had several weeks hauling the nuggars over the Bab-el-Kebir, but we really look upon that place now as matter of fact, having hauled between thirty and forty over; and now there are all these villainous 'Wolseley boats'[i] to get along. Anything more unsuited to the river could not have been devised, but of course, in spite of the soldiers bringing them along themselves *we* have the job, and when in smooth water at Sarras we turn them over. I fear the expedition by these boats will be slow, but all this time Lord Wolseley has been at Wady Halfa he has, no doubt, matured his plans.

We have fifty-three boats in our camp at this moment, to be moved on when the present supply of nuggars is over. More disgraceful boats I never saw, old hulls, leaky, sails frequently in shreds, yards sprung (nearly broken), some without rudders, others without masts; so we had ample opportunities of dismantling the wrecks to get the lame ducks along. The weather has been much cooler of late, and at night pleasantly cold, at least before dawn; but a week ago we had a series of sand-storms, and on our return, almost blinded and pitch dark, I found on two successive nights my tent blown down, and last night half the camp was on the ground, and it poured with rain for an hour or so. When it subsided the air was simply perfect, but the dust had found its way in everywhere. The flies are fewer than they were, for at one time they were simply maddening; fortunately so far there are no mosquitoes, so we have undisturbed nights.

All the generals have been up here (eight miles in length) watching the work going on, and Lord Wolseley expressed himself pleased. In August, when we asked for soldiers to do some of the pulling, it was said they couldn't do work from 10 to 3, too hot. Our routine till a week ago was 5 a.m. turn out; 6 march off – (a few times left camp at 5 a.m.) – six miles along loose sand, get boats hauled up bad places, march back at dark, dine and turn in. Yet not entitled to military allowance! But I fancy we shall get it eventually. Lord C. Beresford is going to take the matter up, and so it ought to be.

1. Oxenham – This letter is written in pencil, but quite clearly.

Sandstorm on the Nile. Taken August 1884, probably while the Naval Brigade sailed up the Nile, boarding the SS *Benhah* off Keneh on 19 August, disembarking at Wady Halfa on the 25th.

Mr A. Pigott (the day after reading of 'Another Failure at the Cataract') and F.H. Pollen enduring the plague of flies, 2 October 1884. Original sketch for images 3 and 4 of *Illustrated London News* front cover, 1 November 1884. See page 69.

We now work fewer hours, for every one would have been played out shortly; we leave at 7 a.m., and get back by 6.30 or 7 nominally. Yesterday, to save our boots, they sent the 'tars' thirty donkeys to help them along a bit. The guides lost four on the way, rather a bad beginning. Anything more amusing I never saw than the men returning to camp last night, some being shot over the beasts' heads, some dropping off over their tails, some dragging the donkeys along; others had made a clean bolt for the desert, and the tar in his jaded state was quite unable to get them again. I fancy this is how we lost them. The officers have camels now, I am thankful to say, but what saddles! Pollen has been very seedy indeed of late, and so has Dr. May and Pigott with a shocking cough, and now it seems to be my turn; poor food, I suppose, and nothing but hard work, and something disagreed, but the worst of anything going wrong is that there is always the danger of dysentery. One or two of our men are in hospital with it, and ten more sick from various causes. But I hope I shall be all right in another day or so. To-day, for the first time, I have had to remain in camp – the only officer who had held out till now uninterruptedly.

How are you, my dearest mother? I am shocked at doing nothing but talk of self. Do take the greatest care of yourself for all our sakes, and mine specially. How is Margaret – and Gerard? I hope he is well; Everard and Bernard[ii] too. The latter is at Cambridge by this time, I suppose.

Letter 8

Rudolph to his Mother, Laura de Lisle

ABKAR, October 25th, 1884.

[1]I am only writing a few lines to enclose my 'affairs'. I have written everything out quite simply, as also my debts, so by writing to the addresses given, the bills would be found to be nearly correct, and my pay will probably have mounted up to a good deal more than I have put down. I paid off about 30*l.* in the Alexandra, and that was hard enough. … I forget whether I told you what was the matter in my last letter, but I have been laid up the last four days with dysentery, though up to the moment of my getting it, I was never better in my life, and unfortunately worked hard one day afterwards in the sun with it on me. Since I have been laid up, I have taken nothing to give my 'within' perfect rest, and I am now, I trust, nearly all right. But of course here, if one has to knock off meat, there is nothing but a little biscuit to eat. If one had milk one could stop these things at the outset. Most of our men have been knocked down right and left, though so far only one bad case amongst them, caused probably by the weather. In the meanwhile don't go and alarm yourself on my account, for I hope to be about again shortly. Whatever *you* do, do take care of yourself for all our sakes. Lord Wolseley, they say, now leaves his *boats* behind him to come as they can, and pushes on to Dongola for the 28th with mounted infantry.

P.S.—I answered dear old Lady Hillyar's[i] letter yesterday, or rather one written for her by some one else.

1. Oxenham – This letter contains his will, and the rest of it is taken up with minute explanations and directions, showing his considerate and kindly mindfulness of the interests of all concerned ; the 'debts' were very small. See p. 139, Will of Rudolph de Lisle dated 24 October 1844, & Mortuary Card.

Letter 9

Rudolph to his Mother, Laura de Lisle

CAMP OF THE NAVAL BRIGADE, SARRAS,
November 1st, 1884.

How glad I am to be able to write and tell you I am all right again now, for I know how pleased you will be to hear it, especially as I was able to move on with our men here. We are now at the extremity of civilization, and in a few days I suppose we shall be in the desert proper. I was absolutely starved for six days – nothing to eat but a little boiled rice and one cup of soup made out of preserved meat, and not very strengthening. However starvation managed to pull me round, and now I am perfectly well and have been doing my regular duty for some time.

Lord Wolseley said, when he started for Dongola, that the cataract party would follow, for which I am truly thankful; but in the meanwhile we are bundled about from one end of the place to the other. We 'broke camp' three days ago and came on here, where we now are in a very pretty place, and I flatter myself our camp (naval) is the neatest of all, for the military are massing here *en route*. I take it in a few days we shall get our 'Brigade' together ready to move on. We are going with the boats I believe. I hope you saw my sketches (three in number) in the *Illustrated* of October 4th. I have sent several others, but so far they have not put them in. Their own special correspondent came to our camp exceedingly grumpy, and remarked there were nowadays a good many too many officers who sketched, and he was very sick to find I had sent a series of cataract sketches to his paper. But I think he said some had been done without seeing the places, which does all right for the British public.

The Canadian boatmen[i] are very fine fellows and work the boats very well indeed; a pity there are not more of them. One was, however, unfortunately drowned yesterday passing over Semneh Cataract. So after all the tremendous hard work we had, Reed has been and wrecked the *Ghizeh*, and as she had passed the last really bad cataract before Dongola, it is really too sad; fortunately no one was drowned. At extreme low Nile I believe they will be able to put new plates on the hole, and next Nile she will be available, but I trust we shall have finished before next July or August.

By last mail I sent my will, which I trust is not necessary just yet, but might be; anyway, as well to have it made out. … When we were started off we were allowed no cook or servants, so we had to get Arab ones at our own expense, and as we made up our minds to keep a regular mess as long as possible we pay 3*s*. 6d. a day to cover expenses – but there is sure to be a good bill at the end of the business. But anyhow I hope the allowances will cover expenses and I shall be able to remit most of my pay. I hope we shall get the military allowance. … If only one thought there was promotion at the end of this, I shouldn't care a straw about the dollars. I do hope we shall get right on; but I fear we shall only get as far as Merawi, which I take it is as far as the boats will go. I am still hoping we may be able to get a couple of machine-guns, and then we may go on, but we are a very small force unless attached to some regiment, armed as we are with rifles only. I believe a certain number of the Wolseley boats are to be given to us to get along as best we can.

Naval Camp, Sarras, 30 October 1884.

THE ILLUSTRATED LONDON NEWS.

REGISTERED AT THE GENERAL POST-OFFICE FOR TRANSMISSION ABROAD.

No. 2376.—VOL. LXXXV. SATURDAY, NOVEMBER 1, 1884. TWO WHOLE SHEETS SIXPENCE. BY POST, 6½D.

1. Final and successful attempt to get the steamer over the second "gate" of the Cataract.
2. Mr. Webber (boatswain), one of the Cataract party.
3. Mr. A. Pigott (the day after) reading of "Another Failure at the Cataract."
4. The Plague of Flies—Enduring it!
5. First day off duty—R. de Lisle trying to sketch.
6. Crossing a rope bridge to look out for hawsers from the steamer.

SKETCHES BY AN OFFICER OF THE NILE EXPEDITION: AT THE SECOND CATARACT.

Front cover of *Illustrated London News*, 1 November 1884, using six of Rudolph's sketches.

Rudolph's preliminary pencil sketches for the *Ghizeh* collage, which eventually appeared on the front cover of the *Illustrated London News*, 6 December 1884. See page 75.

I take it we shall accompany a detachment of boats; but anyhow, be this all as it may, we have sent in a list of the original cataract party, and they are to be the first to move on. I think it quite possible that Lord Wolseley will send a regiment to undertake the attack on Berber (46th) and, if he hears at Dongola there is no great force outside Khartoum, will move across the desert with the mounted infantry alone.

I have just received your charming letter of the 16th October, and I was indeed delighted to hear you were so well and as active as ever. It was indeed most kind of dear old Lady Hillyar writing to Lord John [Hay] and Lord C. Beresford[ii] about me. … She wrote me a very affectionate letter the other day, or rather one which was written for her, and I promptly answered it. She is really a wonderful old lady. May you be spared to her age and longer. I hope by this time you know I have received all your letters and what pleasure they gave me. I also got a letter from Edwin.[iii] … A good many people think there is trouble brewing in the Transvaal, so likely enough there will be another business when this is over, if nothing occurs elsewhere in the meanwhile.

The plague of flies is diminishing, I am thankful to say, and the weather is comparatively cool in the day, and at night it gets quite cold; before sunrise one finds one's self hauling one's blanket round one. It will be cold enough in the boats. The 38th[iv] move on in a day or two's time if the boats are ready. I fear my letter must be a series of repetitions, for I have had to write it at odd moments. 10 p.m – To-morrow I am off with Commander Hammill to Tanjür Cataract, about fifty miles from here. We are going on camels, starting from Semneh Tuesday morning, to have a look at the 'bad places'. The Nile has gone down 7 feet at that place above, and 2½ feet below, *the* Gate, which means any amount more bad water. I fear a certain number of the boats will be lost *en route*, but one must expect that. Please thank Alice[v] so much for her delightful letter – also for the rosary. The crucifix went to pieces almost at once, but I am going to lash it up.

Letter 10

Rudolph to his Mother, Laura de Lisle

NAVAL CAMP, SARRAS,
November 10th, 1884.

So many thanks for your two last letters. I am so thankful to you for writing so continuously, and I am glad to say lately I have been getting my letters quite regularly. You have no idea, on a business like this, how one looks forward to getting the mail. One's employment is varied: since up here one has had to fill up holes in a sinking nuggar, repair a boat which would not otherwise float, fit a rudder to a large nuggar, frequently mend my unmentionables, darn my socks till nothing was left except the darning itself, when they too had to be discarded, repair boots, and lastly, make a table and chest or rather shelf for boots and clothes, so that now one's tent is luxurious.

Making a ramp and building a way for launching steam-boats has been our service job of late. We launched two to-day, and another comes to-morrow. The nuggars (river boats) have been wrecked right and left above the Semneh Cataract, and frequently it has been done on purpose, I take it, by the pilots, who want hanging. There are so many boats it is impossible to have our people in all of them, but I confess I think the Lower Nile boats are worthless for the work above, and they are certainly not worth the agony of hauling over the Second Cataract. So far the Wolseley boats have got on fairly well, but they are very much overladen, for they carry 100 days' provisions: and all those comforts one hears so much about in all the papers are not to be opened till Dongola is reached. I fear there will be a certain loss of life going in these boats, but as I stated before they have been very lucky so far, but that is not very far, not having reached Tanjür yet.

I have just returned three days ago from a very pleasant trip with Com. Hammill to Tanjür and back. The first night, after dinner, with a glorious moon (full) I rode out to Semneh and joined Com. Hammill, slept, and after breakfast rode (on camels) by the desert route to Ambigol, had a look at the cataracts, and went to Tanjür, where we expected to find the shipwrecked crew of the 'Ghizeh'. After one hour's search we found them close to the wreck, which is now almost on her broadside close to the shore, and in a very fine house or shed built from the remains of the deck-house of the ship. The walls were of canvas, and adjoining were the officers' quarters, also roofed in, and a floor made with the floats of the paddles. Outside with bars and bits of awning they had made a capital-looking tent. We got to the 'Ghizeh' camp about 8 p.m., having ridden for eleven hours, except half an hour to lunch, but we had capital camels, a good guide, and our interpreter, who proved an excellent cook, and our party was complete. The 'Ghizehs' had managed to save their machine-gun – which will eventually, I fancy, go to the front – all the ammunition and arms, two months' provisions, &c. The kits (clothes, &c) of the lieutenant commanding (Reed) and Keppel[i] were partly lost or destroyed by water, but none of them were in real want. Of course for the first day or two they were in want of proper shelter, but now their house is built they are quite comfortable and have their rations like any of us. They were rather dejected naturally, especially having the wreck in sight, and so close too. But it was the most providential thing how the vessel ever reached her present destination. Had she gone another 150 yards she must have sunk in a wide part of the river and in deep water with a rushing stream and no boat on board, and all would probably have been drowned. As it was the ship was hurried down the stream as she was filling with water. The engines stopped, for the blow knocked a hole through the engine-room, and in a minute the fires were out and the vessel was at the mercy of the waters. She drifted down two miles and a-half nearly, whirled round rocks, sometimes going bow first, at other times stern first, clearing the rocks by the back wash off them, whirling into the eddies, nearly being driven into several small bays, but being whirled out just as they thought themselves getting into safety. At another time they were rushed along by the sides of precipitous rocks, which formed the bank for some 200 yards, almost touching the shore all the way, and lastly swept into the bay where the 'Ghizeh' now is, her rudder hooked up to a rock, and instantly her bow was swept in to the shore; a hawser was at once got out, and there she lay with the water level with her upper deck on one side. For some time it was hoped, as the Nile fell still lower, she might be repaired and floated again next Nile, if not this one for she had only three plates off, under the engine-room. Now, however, she has turned over on her damaged side, and I fear there is little hope or none, of getting her along again.

We spent a pleasant evening with the shipwrecked mariners, and next morning walked out to the scene of the disaster, and then went down to Ambigol in Tyler's[ii] steam pinnace;[iii] picked up our camels and rode down by the banks of the Nile to a village half-way to Semneh, where we had an excellent dinner. Our camel man killed a lamb in our honour, and we had an excellent grill and native bread, waited till the moon rose at 8, and started off again. By moonlight, the river looked lovely; the lights and shades on the steep cliffs, the distant sand hills and ranges looking beautiful in their variety of neutral tints, with groups of date-palms close to the water's edge, and then the reflection on the water – a scene not to be forgotten. Our trip back was much shorter but the road was so bad and steep in places that we had to lead our camels. We reached Semneh about midnight, slept in the tents belonging to a party of our men who are looking out for boats going over the Bab there, and after breakfast rode in here, where we found Pollen had gone down to Gemai with nearly all our men. Colonel Butler[iv] had telegraphed for me, but from my not being on the spot Pollen went, and then the steam-boats came along and so I remained to assist at this job, but I expect in a day or so I shall go down to relieve him.

I was so very glad to hear Gerard had been to Scotland, and though his journey had not proved very remunerative, still it is change of scene which always does one good. I always think it a mistake to stay too long in one place. I often think how much better it would have been if poor Alice had had a change. … I am glad to hear Bernard is doing so well at Cambridge. I think he is a marvellous genius to pick up the violin as he has, but he is a musical genius. What pleasure to other people in society will he give later on! Such things as drawings give pleasure to the person who does them, and may be some little profit, but little or no pleasure to other people except to a devoted parent like you, who always thinks her children are the most perfect in the world.[1] What a pity other people don't think so too! … I am becoming a regular rolling stone, and I doubt whether I should ever be able to settle down, for I am so devoted to travelling and seeing new scenes and places. And in the service there is no doubt in some ways it is a great advantage not to be married, especially if you have to be away for some three years at a time, for somehow in spite of all the prospect of no promotion and final retirement one lives on in the hope of pushing on. At any rate one cannot afford to let the grass grow under one's feet, and this I feel I inherit from you, for energy is a blessing one cannot be too thankful to possess.

1. Oxenham – Rudolph's humility and entire absence of self–consciousness always made him underrate his own powers. Both his drawing and singing were the means of affording great pleasure to many less partial critics than he supposed his mother to be.

Rudolph's original collage of six sketches, five of which were used for the front cover of the 6 December 1884 issue of the *Illustrated London News*.

THE ILLUSTRATED LONDON NEWS

REGISTERED AT THE GENERAL POST-OFFICE FOR TRANSMISSION ABROAD.

No. 2381.—VOL. LXXXV. SATURDAY, DECEMBER 6, 1884. EXTRA WITH SUPPLEMENT SIXPENCE. By Post, 6½d.

1. The wrecked steamer Ghizeh lying aground under the rocks; the house built by the crew above. 2. Upper part of the Tangour Cataract, where the steamer Ghizeh was lost. 3. The steamer sinking fast. 4. Between the reaches at Ambigol: a bad place for the boats. 5. Some of the crew in their house after the wreck.

THE NILE EXPEDITION: DANGERS AND DIFFICULTIES OF THE RIVER PASSAGE.

SKETCHES BY LIEUTENANT R. DE LISLE, R.N.

The front cover of the 6 December 1884 issue of the *Illustrated London News*.

Colonel Butler's tent, 15 November 1884, Gemai.

Letter 11

Rudolph to his Mother, Laura de Lisle

NAVAL CAMP, GEMAI,
November 20th, 1884.

So many thanks for your letter of the 30th October, which I received yesterday, but which I should have got two days sooner had I been at Sarras instead of at this place. I came down here a week ago to relieve Pollen, who, I am grieved to say, is down with a bad attack of fever and so ill that the doctors will not allow any one to see him. However, I am going down if possible to-morrow to see him. From what I hear I fear he will go no further with us, unless he recovers remarkably quickly, but any one is liable to it, if not here, higher up, and it is better for him to be laid up where he can get hospital treatment, instead of in a boat, where nothing could be done for anyone.

The 38th have lost another boat and the mess sergeant with her; the colonel lost all his gear (clothes, etc.). I am sorry to say one of our men died of fever yesterday at Halfa; he only went to hospital three days before, and it was supposed he would be all right in a few days, but, poor fellow, it was otherwise. He was at my quarters in the Alexandra, and a very smart nice fellow; one of our best men up here. Two other men were also buried yesterday. One company came up here 57 strong; when they left Cairo they were nearly 100, but were eliminated in various ways down to the above number—rather a bad beginning before getting to the point. We of course get all sorts of rumours, but your news is probably more authentic, so I won't say much on that score, beyond that the Mahdi is on the move and also Osman Digna,[i] who fought us in the Soudan in the early part of the year. Now they have gathered their crops there is every reason, if so inclined, why they should move, and the Mahdi, if he is to keep up his reputation, will have to do something. I hear from Captain Rawson[ii] from time to time, and he told me in his last letter received yesterday, that the 'friendlies' at Suakim finding we were doing nothing have changed sides, and they have been armed by us.

At the Cape too matters are looking very serious, and to think the whole of all these things might have been avoided if only the Government had shown a little firmness or even had a policy of some sort. … Lord Wolseley rode down from Dongola by camel a few days ago, had a conversation with the chief of his staff, and returned at once. He rode down in three and a-half days, about fifty-two miles a day, splendid going over this benighted country. I was dining that evening at the Canadian camp, and as soon as the train arrived bringing his lordship, they made up their minds to give him a reception, and in less time that it takes to write this they made a huge bonfire and closed round their fire and began singing part-songs wonderfully well, and as he passed they cheered him. He looked out of the window and waved to them and seemed much pleased; a very picturesque scene it made. I was much amused with what you said about the sketch of October 25th, but I must say I was disgusted with the sketches as reproduced of November 1st. In the first place blue-jackets do not wear waistcoats and look as the men represented in the *Illustrated* did. Coki, the sheik, was an excellent reproduction, and exactly like him; but not so Poore[iii] and the others of November 1st—very poor.

Crossing a rope bridge on the hawsers for the steamer. Used as part of the front cover, *Illustrated London News*, 1 November 1884. See page 69.

Original sketches of Lt. Poore RN and Coki. Used as part of the front cover, *Illustrated London News*, 25 October 1884. See page 115.

R. de Lisle trying to sketch (first day off duty); F. Pollen driven to extremities; A. Pigott philosophical. The sketch of Rudolph only was used as image 5 on the front cover of the *Illustrated London News*, 1 November 1884.

I made what I thought a good group, and they made three separate sketches of it. … I have been employed getting whalers repaired and refitted, but there is a man senior to me here, so I have only a secondary job. I am looking out especially to the fitting out of the Naval Brigade boats, and I trust we shall soon have a chance of moving on in them. The troops are passing through now pretty fast, taking boats from here. Where we had a day or two ago 246, now there are about 180. The only thing I fear is that when the Staff see the naval boats they will covet their neighbours' goods and appropriate them; for this reason I have them nearly a mile and a-half from the upper end of the reach, to be out of sight as much as possible.

The work here is continuous, but easy: turn out at 6, and work till 8 a.m.; hour for breakfast, wash, etc.; work till 12.30; dinner till 2; then work till dark, 5.40. The times are easy therefore, and the weather usually pleasant and quite cold at night, which is a blessing, but the last few days have been very hot again and very little wind.

All the home news you gave me interested me very much; in fact little bits of news of that sort interest me almost more than anything else. How I wish I had had more opportunities of cultivating music so as to be able to play one's own accompaniments, but, do you remember, in '71 I had a chance of lessons and did not take them? We had a piano on the Alexandra and I was beginning to be able to play a few pieces, or rather accompaniments, and then this business came on, and of course one is out of it again; still I hope, if only for one's own amusement, to have a chance of strumming away again. … I was so glad to hear Gerard had had a day's shooting at the Outwoods.[iv] I wish he could get many days. I spoke about him to some of the Canadian officers, and they said, one and all, he was sure to succeed; but any way, if he is happy that is the great thing, and after all, this is first-rate experience for him. I hope indeed this has been a good year for him, for by the papers it has been an excellent year [for the harvest] taking it all round. Last Sunday I heard Mass at the Canadian camp, just like Brittany over again. They (the *voyageurs*) sang throughout, and very well indeed – in unison. The altar was in a tent open to the front, round which we were assembled. The men who attended were most devout in spite of a certain amount of noise outside.

Letter 12

Rudolph to his Mother, Laura de Lisle

NAVAL CAMP, GEMAI,
November 30th, 1884.

So many thanks for your letters of the 6th and 13th inst., the latter just received. I was unable to write sooner, as we have been having a lot of finicking work with the boats, getting the soldiers on. They are not getting on as fast as the authorities expected, and the sick list is very heavy; at Halfa there are no less than 300 down, and as I think I told you in my last letter, Pollen has been seriously ill at Halfa, but I trust he is now going on as satisfactorily as possible. I went in to see him a couple of days ago, and found him very weak; I fear there is no chance of his going on. But really the rumours one hears are nothing short of amusing, so preposterous they are at times. … I hear that Lord Charles Beresford told an officer to-day he should try and get me on. Without the Alexandra's and Monarch's – in other words the Cataract party, there would have been no Naval Brigade at all. … Since coming here I have been fitting out the boats for the Naval Brigade, which are now increased to fourteen boats. We have ten ready, and the others within a few days, but the Naval Brigade will not move on till they have finished with us. Without the blue-jackets what they would have done fitting the boats out I can't think; so we shall probably remain till all the boats and troops are gone on.

The river is getting lower and lower, and now we can hardly recognise the water. The Naval Camp at Abkar looks another place altogether, and instead of swift streams it is a mass of mud and sluggish water, but not so higher up, where the water is getting bad for boats on account of the rocks and bad places for 'tracking' the boats along, and the proof of it is, the slowness with which the troops get on. The 38th left here on the 6th of this month, and are only just past Dal, seventy-two miles from here.

Since I last wrote another *voyageur* and one Krooman[i] have been drowned, both of them near Ambigol, and a private who was in the boat when she swamped managed to get hold of a biscuit-box and floated down nearly three miles before he could reach the shore.

I fear your fond hopes for my promotion are simply beside the question, and in a very short time the cataract work will all have been forgotten, and it will be hardly a claim, and once these senior men are put in, one's chance is a very small one indeed, if there is even that to look forward to; but one can only do one thing, that is one's duty whatever it is, and something might turn up some day.

I hear the Alexandra has returned to Malta, where she will probably remain for the winter. I should certainly have been very much disgusted had I been there for the winter and no shooting again, but one generally manages to make the most of any place. When we first came up here we thought it quite a novelty sleeping in a tent; now it will be on the ground and no tent, but after tracking and pulling all day one will not be very particular; one gets completely out of the way of pillows and sheets, etc., and sand makes a comfortable bed. One good thing about this country is that there is no rain, otherwise rheumatism would be rife as well as fever and dysentery. Several officers have already gone back on account of the latter. It is astonishing how it pulls people down.

One piece of news in your last letter gave me some reassurance, viz., that Lord John Hay is good enough to have his eye on me. He is pretty sure to be at the Admiralty when his command in the Mediterranean is over. I trust he will remain the full three years and then one may have a chance of finishing the commission under him; he has always been very kind to me. Captain Rawson is the pleasantest captain I have ever served under – too good I sometimes think, for one will feel the difference with another later on.

You will be glad to hear I had a chance of hearing Mass to-day and last Sunday at the Canadian camp. The Père Bouchard[ii] is a man who has seen the world, and profited by it, for he understands men. He was two years in Khartoum, and another at El-Obeid and beyond, and knows the Mahdi. The Canadians are a very hard-working lot of men. Curiously enough amongst them is an old friend of mine, John Windham,[iii] who at one time was a 'mid' with me. He has indeed had a chequered life, and is certainly one of the best of the *voyageurs*. I had him to dinner before he went on, and he told me all last winter in Manitoba he had been working with his pick and shovel on the new Canadian railway. I hope he will have better days. I frequently yarn with the Canadians, and I get any amount of work out of them, and they insist occasionally upon my accepting some of their excellent tobacco, which is the most acceptable thing one can get. Some people don't get on with them; some of the *Club* soldiers don't understand their free and easy ways. I would give anything to have a trip to Manitoba and Three Rivers one of these days, but the same grim impediment always stands in one's way.

You will be glad to hear I kept my birthday last Sunday as you would wish, for I went to Holy Communion, as did numbers of the Canadians.[1] The altar was in a tent amongst the palm-trees, and the men all stood round in a semicircle and sang, and very well too, different parts in unison; altogether a very picturesque sight. Outside were Arabs, who hovered round, and, as is their custom, jabbered away. I nearly ran at them, but after a while they moved off. The Canadians have already lost four men, three by drowning and a fourth from a fall. At best so far this is rather a cold-blooded kind of game.

We are astonished to hear by telegram that the Bechuanaland question is finished, and that the Boers have given in; but what about the brutal murder of Mr. Bethell,[iv] the Government Commissioner? I suppose they have forgotten all about him. … So many thanks for thinking of the wedding present for Cecily Feilding.[v] Please send her the cross and necklace with my best love and wishes for her happiness, but that is certain, for he is such a nice fellow. So glad Bernard enjoys his university career so much; it will do him no end of good; also that Freda[vi] has such a nice house, where I trust she will have a chance of entertaining me some day. … Delighted to hear Gerard is not getting ruined over his farm. I wish I was in England to buy you a new pony, for 'Fairy' is played out.

1. Oxenham – It appears from a statement of the Abbé Bouchard's, already quoted that he again went to Confession and Holy Communion—his last Communion—on Sunday, 7 December, and heard Mass for the last time on Monday, 8 December, the feast of the Immaculate Conception.

Letter 13

Rudolph to his Mother, Laura de Lisle

NAVAL CAMP, GEMAI,
December 6th, 1884.

This is probably the last letter *in ink* you will receive from me for some time, for the first half of the Naval Brigade go forward on Tuesday next, viz., the Cataract party, and I am sure we have to thank Lord John Hay for it. … In time one of our party found means of telegraphing to the ship and letting him know, and I feel convinced that it is owing to the orders he sent to Captain Boardman[i] that we are now going on. The life of our party, Pollen, I am grieved to say, has been very ill indeed – enteric, if not typhoid fever, and is now very weak, but I sincerely trust out of danger. Still I fear there is no chance of his eventually joining us, but I am glad to say he will get his promotion anyhow, whether he comes on or not. The difficulties of the river are, as Lord Wolseley says, *immense*, and his Address, which was publicly read in camp, is one to stimulate every one to do his utmost; but at the Cataract of Ambigol there are no less than 170 boats unable to get along, and further up the Cataract of Dal is reported to be closed. Everywhere nearly we have to carry overland all stores, etc., and it is said the boats also, in one or two of the worst places, but I fancy the 'Navy' will manage to find water in the rapids to float them – of one thing you may be sure, they will do their very utmost. Nearly one hundred boats have reached this place, and without sails, so we have been hard at it making new ones, as many as possible in the time; fortunately, I think there will be no necessity for sails at present, for the last fifty boats, as they have not men to man them. The 75th Highlanders[ii] and the 18th R. Irish[iii] go on in the next few days, and then the 79th,[iv] one or two companies, and then the whole business maybe termed 'in motion'. The second half of the Naval Brigade follows a week or ten days later, I believe; but I am thankful I am going on with our party, especially after having fitted out every boat for them (N. Brigade).

December 7th. To–day has been the busiest day we have had for some time, and Lord Charles Beresford started off with two boats to Dal, to see the cause of the block, and returns in about a week or eight days, I believe, and will come on with the second half; some of the 75th left, and a number of natives for transport service. The latter are fairly good for the ordinary stream, but lose their heads at once in the rapids, which is absolutely fatal. Another solider was picked up (his remains) at Semneh, eleven already; there will be many more before it is finished. The *voyageurs* have lost four, not five, as I said in my last letter, but they are not at all pleased with the river. If only the government had been able to make their minds up sooner, what a lot of lives would have been saved, and the expedition, instead of being just on the move, would have been well on for Khartoum by this time. We (Naval Brigade) are starting very late, but I am hoping we shall do the distance in the best time, and so we ought, if they had not thought fit to put in all kinds of stores with the usual remark – 'the Navy always manage all right' – and so they have continued until the last straw in on the camel's back. I trust the weight will not prove too much. We have to portage everything in several places, so all this extra weight will tell terribly against the time we take, for this item will not be taken into account when we arrive at Dongola. The authorities expect a brush at Merawi, so I trust we shall get up in time. If it is possible we certainly shall.

The 42nd have worked night and day in one or two places to get by the block, determined to get on, and so far have done remarkably well. One or two regiments have done equally unsatisfactorily – as far as the boats are concerned; but I have no doubt should there be a brush on the river one of these regiments (38th) will do very well, for they are a fine set of men, and their fault seems to be their unacquaintance with a boat.

I managed to get to Mass to-day (Sunday) in spite of all the boats going away, with the result I remained filthy all day, not having my usual swim in the Nile. I am very glad indeed having been able to get to Mass. Since being here, and in more ways than one, it has turned up trumps, for I have met several of the swells, and I am glad to say manage to hit it off capitally with the soldiers commanding. Nothing could have been nicer than Colonel Grove[v] all the time we have been here, and the result is that we have been working our very utmost. To-day the soldiers 'stood off', being Sunday, but not so the tars, for I kept them making sails, etc., till sunset, and they grasped the idea and worked well, but then they expect to have to work, if possible, harder on Sundays than other days. We have Pollen and ten men in hospital, and one man moon blind,[vi] so we are a good deal reduced from what we ought to be. We were nearly 70 in the 'cataract party' when we left, and now all we can get together from various casualties is 42 (without officers).

This expedition, owing chiefly I take it to the absence of vegetables – for we only get onions (very few) once in a way – and living upon preserved meat, will lose most men by sickness, and exposure, through getting wet, etc., tracking the boats along; by drowning in the cataracts; and thirdly, I fancy, by the part they are sent up here to play. Of course if the boats return fairly empty instead of being crowded up, so many casualties will not occur. If the whole business lasts into April, I see every prospect of *very* short rations, and if beyond, which seems certain unless many more camels are bought.

Letter 14

Rudolph to his Mother, Laura de Lisle

NAVAL BRIGADE CAMP, AMBIGOL,
December 14th, 1884.

This may be the last time for a day or two I shall have a chance of writing, for here we are with the cataract party fighting our way up the Nile, and a fight it is. So far, thank God, we have had no casualties, and we are through Sarras, Semneh, Wady-a-Teir, and the lower part of Ambigol; and to-morrow it is a hard piece of cataract to do – so much so that we have to take everything out and portage overland. The next two days will be eventful ones, and then D.V. we shall be on the way to Dal, where everything will have to be taken out again, and *boats* and everything carried overland two miles up a hill, but I have no doubt we shall find means of doing this also. Anyhow, yesterday we took the wrong passage, and it was impossible to go back, so we stood on, and fortunately had a good breeze, or we should have been in rather a 'quandary'. We set a regular cloud of canvas, and every one is delighted with the boats I selected and their fittings. I had all the sails enlarged, and fitted up the boats like men-of-war boats, and it is really a beautiful sight seeing the boats driving along.

In innumerable places, where the water, owing to rocks and the rush of the stream, is irresistible, we track through and take every precaution – sometimes fifty men on a rope to haul each boat through in succession – and till last night we were all in one camp together. Every boat has its tent and cooking materials, &c., so when it is getting dark we stop, secure for the night, and pitch our tents, which are double bell tents and most comfortable. Last night, unfortunately, the two boats which had gone up the right passage had our tea and coffee, so most had to go without – but I had a private stock of my own stowed away for the officers and my boat's crew – so they got rum instead. Even when the boats were very deep in the water we determined to take that one, but in a month that will be finished, and I take it is not likely to be replenished. Our officers are Pigott, Lieut. R.N., in command; I am second in command, Munro, Sub-Lieut., and a capital man,[i] and Mr. Webber,[ii] boatswain of the Monarch.

Mr Webber, boatswain and one of the cataract party. Used as part of the front cover of the *Illustrated London News*, 1 November 1884. See page 69.

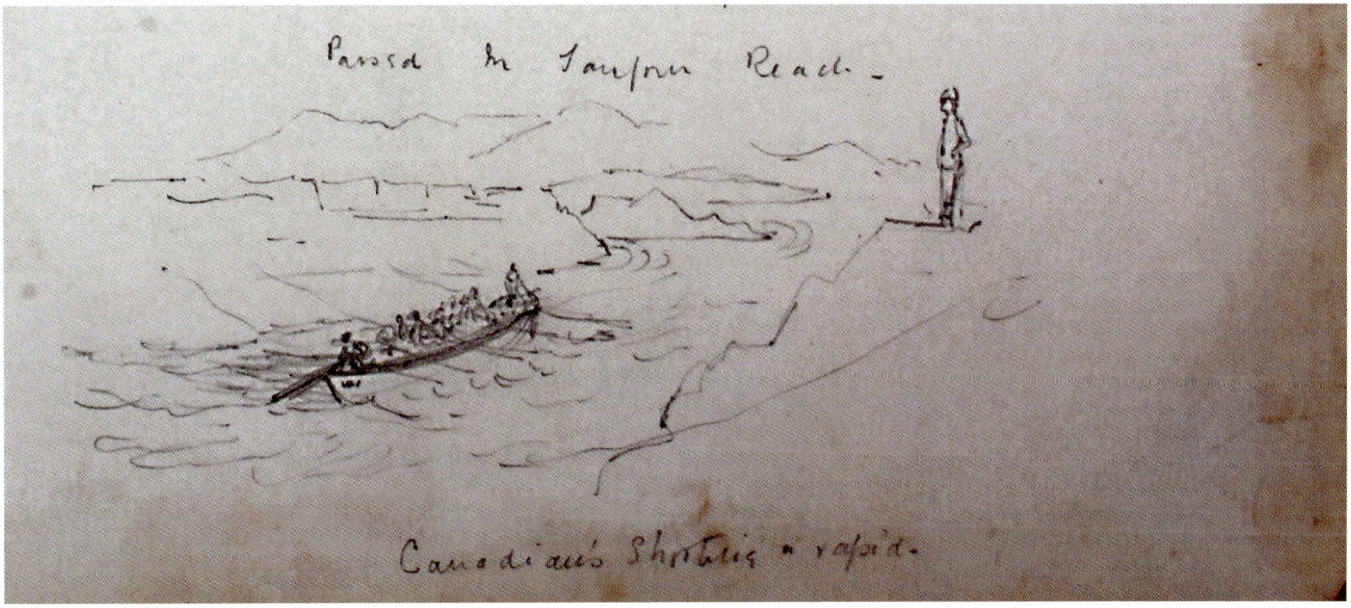

Canadians shooting the rapids.

We have 45 blue-jackets, 2 stokers, 2 engine-room artificers, 1 carpenter, 1 interpreter – an Egyptian who speaks excellent French, so he is in my boat; and he is a cook into the bargain, and works like a horse when we are tracking along. Besides the usual weights carried in the boats by troops, we have one Gardner Gun and 8,000 rounds of ammunition for it, and altogether about 3½ tons extra weight; and then we have no Canadians in our boats. So far 28 people have been drowned; the *voyageurs* have already lost six. To-day here they were shooting the rapid reach, and they struck a rock, boat smashed to pieces, and another poor fellow was drowned. A blue-jacket with a Canadian crew dropped down the stream, and made an attempt to get off a man who was pitched on to a rock, and failed, had to cut their rope, and were themselves shot down; the next attempt was successful, and the man's life was saved. The Canadians were so pleased that they passed the hat round, and gave Stevens[iii] a very handsome present for his gallant rescue; he was steering, and I am glad to say it has been officially rewarded. Anybody who can see what the river now is would appreciate what the rescue was. We arrived here after the affair had occurred. The man is coxswain of a steam pinnace here plying on this reach, which is now too bad for her to move further up. Through all the rapids, etc., except when tracking, the officers of course steer, but it is amusing to hear the soldiers talk about how of course the sailors know all about rapids, etc., as if ships went over rocks, shooting rapids, etc., every day of their lives.

I got a hole knocked in my boat the day before yesterday, and she leaked so badly that when we arrived at Semneh we had to haul her up and repair her, and your devoted son did the carpentering; and, in fact, now we have got quite into the way of doing several little odd jobs besides sailoring. I am going to make shoes when we are through the worst parts. To me, I may say, it is wonderful how the soldiers got through at all, and it's marvellous there has been so little loss of life. I only wish we had had a chance of moving on three weeks ago, for the river gets lower and lower and rocks crop up

Third rapid below Semneh, 11 December 1884.

everywhere; an instant's hesitation in a bad place would probably be fatal to everyone in the boat, but the soldiers work splendidly and tremendously hard. They have 10 men in a boat, and we have 7 on an average, so of course it is harder work for the blue jackets when tracking, and rowing too, for our boats are much heavier. But I am glad to say the 'Blues' are working splendidly , and D.V. I trust we shall get along all right.

The return journey is another matter, speaking only of the river. In July when the Nile is high, and better still in August, it merely requires nerve to shoot the rapids, but if the expedition is over before, and the return journey is in boats, I fear the loss of life will be very much greater; but after all, that is one of the extra risks of this expedition over any other. Our orders are *not* to stop at Dongola, but go straight on as fast as possible to Ambucol, near Merawi, and from there something is to be undertaken. We are bringing all necessary paraphernalia with us, and so we are sure if we arrive safely to go straight on to the front. The 42nd Highlanders are glorious fellows; every one knows what they are when fighting, and now to see them on the river is a sight – full of go and determination to overcome the dangers of the river. Their officers are splendid fellows, for at the best for them the work is not theirs, and I am glad to say they are beating every one except the Naval Brigade. Our experience with steamers and nuggars has proved simply invaluable; had they changed the officers who commanded the men on the 2nd Cataract, the men would not have had the confidence they have now. We form the first half of the Naval Brigade; the second comes on in a few days. I fancy, when they have collected the blue-jackets who are to form it, Lord C. Beresford will, when we meet, command the lot.

Hammill hauled our boats over Semneh, where he now is, and he looked very much cut up when he saw us starting without him. He entertained us at Semneh *en route*. All those choice provisions the papers were so full of for the expedition are not to be touched before Dongola, and many boats *never* touch them, as their mangled remains on the rocks show. I wish you could see me scribbling this letter, my sketch-book the table, which accounts for the ghastly writing, and now, 11p.m. the only time to write; but there is a post going out to-morrow, so I determined, having arrived at a post, to start in and write a disjointed letter to you, as you are about as fond of getting letters from me as I am from you. [some sketches are introduced here.]

Some of the places were very narrow, and the water simply boiling, but we are through, I am thankful to say. I must thank you more than I can say for your great kindness in writing so often. I have received all your letters so far. Do take the greatest care of yourself for all our sakes, and give my love to all. I hope to write again higher up shortly. If only we can get above Dal, I trust we shall rattle on in the smooth water we have for 80 miles.

Letter 15

Rudolph to his Mother, Laura de Lisle

SARKAMATTO, ABOVE DAL,
December 20th, 11 p.m.

A short letter this time to tell you we have reached this place safely and without accident in 10 days; the most momentous I have ever spent in my life. And to-day has been a thrilling one, bringing our boats through Dal; the slightest mistake anywhere, and 'mafeesh', as they say in this country. We brought our boats through with everything out, and ten men pulling, and were favoured with a fresh breeze; got through the first four, then walked back and brought through the remaining three. We steered the boats of course ourselves, and never were the crews nearer 'kingdom come'. I take it that to-day's was a place where, if a boat came to grief, there was little or no chance of approaching her to bring off the crew. Lord Charles Beresford did pilot, having been through with a crew of Canadians once before. We tried it yesterday, and nearly lost a boat; no wind, and for the first time the Navy were beaten; had to find our way back, and did so in safety, 490 [his own number], I am glad to say, having the place of honour, to fish out the way back as leader. Anyhow we got back all right, and to-day with the breeze we got all our boats through; waded up again, for everything was portaged about 3 miles, and off we started again and reached this spot, where we have taken in 14 days more provisions *en route* for Dongola.

Personally I am rather a wreck, hands skinned all over and like raw beef, and arms nearly ditto, feet cut about over the rocks, and thorns in them; so I am lame also, in fact what Amo [Ambrose] would have called a poor creature. But I am thankful to say I got knocked about by hanging on to a rope let go by 3 blue-jackets, and got dragged over rocks into the water; but the boat was saved, so it was all right. To give you an idea of the kind of work it is through Dal, not a soldier goes through without 6 *voyageurs*, and most boats are pulled and sailed through by them entirely. They are astonished how our deeply-laden boats get along, and have got here in 10 days. They are simply invaluable to the soldiers, and are surprised how we have got along without them, but the 'nuggar' experience has proved invaluable. Still there are innumerable 'breakers ahead', and we are not out of this business yet; 10 or 12 miles from here there are 6 miles of treacherous bad water, and more boats have come to grief than people know of. One company between Ambigol and Amara (above here) lost 6 out of 8 boats; another company 4 out of 10, and all their arms and ammunition; and all along the way one sees wreck after wreck. It is astonishing how few lives have been lost considering the magnitude of the work to be overcome; and it is astounding to me how the soldiers get along at all. Without the *voyageurs* they would not, or very few of them would, succeed. But the pluck of the 42nd Highlanders and the 75th – the former were so keen that they actually started without *voyageurs* – I think beyond praise. Unfortunately we led one company above Semneh wrong, for we took the wrong passage, could not get back, and only got through ourselves with very considerable difficulty. How they have managed I can't think, but I trust all right. The 75th have got on wonderfully well also, and will have the place of honour in the field. The other unfortunate regiments are to be left behind to garrison *en route* on account of having lost so many boats. But if we come back by water not many of us will return, unless it is a high Nile, for the water changes so much and the first mistake, getting caught by an eddy, must be fatal. Providence has certainly looked after us well, and backed up our utmost efforts together with taking every human precaution; still we can't say too much till above Amara. The scenery between Tanjore and Dal is really lovely, the first really beautiful scenery I have seen; high hills—for they are hardly mountains—perhaps 2,000 feet high; the blue and purple hills—for it is only when close to them that one sees how ghastly and barren they are—the green banks with here and there a cluster of palm-trees and patches of vegetation close to the banks, make a picture which, if I return, I hope to be able to give some idea of, if unable to give a just idea of the atmosphere.

The climate now is very good, and I think better than lower down, but the nights are really very cold indeed; last night we were cut off from our bedding, etc., on account of having sent everything on by camels to the other end of the Cataract, 3 miles distant. The men we got under cover with a very fair house I built with boats, sails, and biscuit–boxes, but Pigott and I slept as we were (or tried to) in the open. I had a baddish cough from being continually in the water before, and the freezing has cured it, and glad I was when daylight arrived, and away we started. Some of the troops have taken 28 days getting here, but I fear several of our men are knocked up, and no wonder if you knew what they have been having to go through; but there it is, we must get along somehow!

I wish indeed Pollen was with us, for he was always so bright and cheery till knocked down by that wretched fever, and poor fellow, had he come along, there is no telling what might not have been his fate. You must excuse the writing, as my hands are such that I can hardly hold the pen, but dont go and alarm yourself, for one of these days, when I can give them a little rest, they will get all right.[1] My feet are the most troublesome, but I am horribly egotistical in giving you all these details always of self. And to think I should have never wished you the usual Christmas greetings, but if I have not done so in writing, you know well how I have wished you and all every happiness and blessing. We *are* preparing for 'peace and goodwill'! But I trust most heartily, my dearest mother, you and all are very well, and [you are] taking the greatest care of yourself for all our sakes, and I wish you many, many happy returns of the new year. The same to all your party; I mean Alice, etc., and the Welds[i] and Gwenny.[ii] I have been intending to write to her, and tell her from me that her scapular the other day was my only article of clothing when I swam on shore through a bit of a rapid with a line to get our boats round an 'awkward corner!' I wasn't quite sure I should reach, but fortunately did, and we hauled the boats round. How is Margaret?[iii] I wish she would write, and in ink, for up here, as you may imagine, letters and papers are much appreciated when received, for we have no books or time to read them. The water was so bad near the scenery I before alluded to, that I was only able to make a few rough sketches, and my hands prevent my doing much, or writing more this time.

P.S.—Five large crocodiles seen two days ago—not by me, however.

1. Oxenham – The apology was not needed. All his letters to the last are written in the same clear and beautiful hand, though the punctuation, and sometimes the construction, is apt to be a little casual, as was under the circumstances almost inevitable. The marvel is that there should be so very little of this kind to correct.

Christmas sketches taken 23–24 December 1884.

Camp, Christmas Day 1884.

Rudolph's final three letters were received by his mother, Laura, in the weeks after she had been informed – by telegram – of his death at Abu Klea on 17 January 1885

R.I.P.

Letter 16

Rudolph to his Mother, Laura de Lisle

NAVAL BRIGADE, 70 MILES ABOVE DONGOLA,
January 1st, 1885.

We are now progressing rapidly, passing boats right and left which left ages before we did, and we are now doing an average of 22 miles a day against the stream, which is strong in places; but there are no cataracts, and it is heavenly work sailing along under every stitch of canvas as we did to-day, and made good 32 miles; had the same breeze lasted all day, we should have probably made 45 miles, but unfortunately it fell light during the afternoon. We started by moonlight and finished an hour after sunset, so as you may imagine we are not letting the grass grow under our feet. We passed two of the soldiers' boats dismasted and in a helpless state; no idea of how to repair damages. It is astonishing the ignorance of some of these gallant troops when they get into difficulties, but perhaps very much more astonishing how they got through the cataracts at all. It seems now like a dream, for now we have delightful times sailing along; hard work too, for we have to pull and track when the wind falls light, for we cannot 'tarry by the way'; but there are few or hardly any rocks and only sand-banks and shoals to look out for; occasionally we touch, but soon get our boats off again. And the last three days on the river our boats must have been a picture, with all sail set and even waterproof sheets turned to account, and fortunately turned to better use.

We are all anxiously looking forward to receiving a pile of letters when we arrive at Debbeh or Ambucol, and there seems little doubt we are going across the desert to Khartoum; – a mere handful, so they say, for it seems to me the regiments are scattered all over the river; but of course the camel corps will be on the spot and at least two regiments. I hope the 100 marines and ourselves will be together; they are glorious fellows, and the backbone of the country. We heard to-day the advance would not take place till next full moon; I trust it is not true. The weather now is splendid, cold at nights, and our men on the whole better than they have been; but how we shall get on across a fiery desert on a pint of water remains to be seen, but with luck 170 miles, unless all the wells are defended, ought to take not more than 12 or 14 days. Camels will carry the water, and we shall have our arms and Gardner Gun to drag along. We ought to be at Debbeh on the 3rd with luck, and Ambucol is only 40 miles beyond, but the river takes an ugly turn making the prevailing wind foul, so we shall have to pull against a strong breeze and current for a few miles, but possibly the wind may follow the course of the stream.

We met our old friend the Nassif Kheir a couple of days ago towing nuggars. She informed us she had orders to tow us up to Ambucol, but she had to put in to Dongola for wood, so I trust she will never catch us, as we are most anxious to do the whole journey unaided, and with all the helpless boats on the river it would be very hard lines on the soldiers. All our watches have run down, and we have the greatest difficulty in waking at the right time, but as I look out for waking up the camp, they sometimes find themselves up an hour or so too soon but never too late. We breakfast by starlight, but you have no idea what a wonderful boat equipment we have, tents, cooking gear, and everything which contributes to comfort, and all provided with most wonderful forethought on the part of Col. Butler and others who had to think the matter out. Our Nile stores, 90 days, are intact, and I believe we are the only party which can boast the same; in many cases they have been broken into, and bacon, etc., and medical comforts used, viz., three bottles of brandy, etc.; they will get skinned, but we made a matter of honour that nothing should be touched, and had men at all the portages to look thoroughly well after the niggers who carried it, and only a few private articles were lost, which I call wonderful considering the amount of carrying at different points there was to be done.

I want you kindly to get me two watches, *nickel*, from the Midland Watch-making Company;[i] they cost 25s. each, and would be of infinite use perhaps later on, and if not they are not of any very great expense. I unfortunately lost all my gold out of one of my pockets, when stripping to carry a line ashore for our boats; it was all I had, £4, but after all one doesn't much want money, and I have managed to pick up a few eggs on the way with the remaining piastres (2½*d.*) I had. But the provisions are more than enough, and naturally I eat hardly any meat here, but rice and preserved potato, soup made out of the tinned meat, and tea and coffee, and I am thankful to say I have been wonderfully well, thank God! No one knows what we went through getting up as far as Hannek, but here we are providentially all right, and without a casualty of any sort, and our boats in thorough good repair. I trust you will be able to read my shocking writing, but I am writing in the tent on my knees with a bit of wood this time rigged up as a table.[1] From my heart, my dearest mother, I wish you and all many happy returns of the New Year. We drank all your healths heartily—and may *you* and all be spared for many years to come, and D.V. for me to meet you again later on. We shall know more shortly, but you must not be anxious if you do not hear from me.

1. Oxenham – The letter is written in pencil, but quite clearly.

Letter 17

Rudolph to his Mother, Laura de Lisle

KORTI
January 6th, 1885.

So many thanks for your charming letter of December 10th received to-day, and also please thank Margaret very much for her addition to it, which was most entertaining. I was very glad the *Illustrated* people sent you one or two of the original sketches. I flatter myself they have not the stiffness of their reproductions, still I confess I am sordid enough to wish the editor would communicate with me to my advantage. I wrote rather a peremptory letter last time, asking that the sketches might be sent to you, whether used or not: for I know you would value them, knowing the difficulties under which they were done. The flies are, thank goodness, finished, but for an hour or two before sunset the sand-flies are most annoying, but nothing, I believe, to what they are later on—when the weather gets warmer; though the nights are cool and sometimes quite cold, the days are intensely hot, and to-day is one of the hottest days we have had. We had from Dongola light winds, foul usually, and calms, which meant dragging the boats along as best we could, and yesterday morning the wind was strong and ahead, so we got up at 2 a.m., and started by moonlight for this place which we reached at 7.30 p.m., pitch dark for there was no moon, and right glad we were to have arrived without assistance.

We tracked over bad ground about 27 miles, very strong current against us into the bargain, and we were glad to get our hot tea and turn in: 16½ hours' work, only stopping for about 1¾ altogether from start to finish. Our old friend the Nassif Kheir came up with us 9 miles from here, having been sent down on purpose to tow us up. And we met her first at Dongola, where she was putting in for wood, and expected to pick us up next day, but in spite of head winds, we went as fast as she did, and we did our utmost to get in before her, and she arrived too late to tow us.

Our boats looked in beautiful order as they rode past the 'only General' who stood on the bank, and watched us go by to our (or the boat's) last resting-place, and was much pleased as we tossed our oars as a salute to him as we went by. He remarked how beautifully clean our boats looked, and in as good condition as when we started. To-day we returned all our stores into the Commissariat, and turned our boats over to the authorities, and to-morrow morning we get our ships of the desert, and the morning after start off into the desert with the Guards for Gakdul, 100 miles across the desert, then 90 miles and odd across to Metammeh for Shendy, where we expect D.V. to find some of Gordon's steamers, get on board there, and then try and force our way through to Khartoum. For the Nile being so low there are, no doubt, no end of rapids, and the 6th Cataract stops the way, but we trust to be able to get them along somehow, if they have enough steaming power for the work. If successful, we shall return by steamer, and go right on to Berber, and thence all well, go across the desert again to Suakim through Osman Digna's country, and back by the Red Sea; – that I believe is supposed to be our programme, but who can tell what may happen before that time arrives?

A party starts to-morrow up the river for Merawi, the scene of Stewart's murder,[i] to punish the natives, and bad water they will have to go through. For there are no end of bad places 50 miles beyond this, which extend, so it is said, for 150

The *Nassif Kheir*, 30 December 1884.

miles, and no niggers to drag the steamers over, for above they are no longer friendlies. The General seems sanguine about the result; but all are agreed it is the campaign with the greatest amount of hardship yet encountered by modern soldiers, and when the campaign is over, the dangers are not, for the river has to be encountered again, and for one life lost coming up, I take it 15 or 20 will be lost at least going down; for at low Nile in the bad water, going a tremendous speed with the current, it is impossible to see a rock till almost on the top of it, and then the slightest error will prove fatal, probably to all in the boat. If he (Lord Wolseley) is wise, I think he will not endeavour to send the whole expedition down by the water, but of course he may look upon the expected loss as one of the items of the campaign.

There is now a very large camp indeed here, and one is smothered by the dust and heat, and thousands of camels (perhaps 2,000 or 3,000), baggage animals and running camels, but I fear our 'mounts' will be very poor, as most of the good animals have been appropriated, and the remainder have sore backs and generally weak, but I suppose we shall get them along somehow. Our boats we managed to repair when they required it, but I fear sheets of tin and white lead and tacks will hardly put our old camels to rights. My next letter will probably be from across the desert, that is if it ever reaches, for it is likely enough it maybe cut off, so I shall write short letters probably, and send them whenever there is a chance. We are going to make a rush across the desert if the animals do not collapse on the way. There are some prisoners in the camp, taken at Gakdul; laden they were, or their camels rather, with dates for the Mahdi, and one unfortunately escaped, so the Mahdi will probably get a note of warning before our arrival, but they all seemed utterly surprised at the General taking this route, and fully expected us to have gone *viâ* Debbeh instead, which is the main route, where we should have been opposed. Lord Wolseley keeps his plan to himself, and there perhaps he is wise.

The second half of the Naval Brigade are close upon us, and from what we can hear they are beating our time coming up; most creditable to them, but they got better winds, which means a great deal, and after leaving Hannek, we expected strong fair winds and proper picnic times, [but had] instead no winds, or foul ones, and hard work all the way – most disappointing, for I had intended working up a good many sketches, and of course never had a moment to spare. My hands, I am glad to say, are gradually getting all right again, but will be scarred for life all over; but on these sort of trips if one gets back at all one is very lucky with a whole skin. There are a good many sick here, chiefly from dysentery and fever, but most of the more weakly men fell out and were left in hospitals on the way through the cataracts, and on the whole the state of health is good; all our boats and men were perfectly sound when we arrived, which was a great blessing, but hands and feet a good deal knocked about, and a good many boots were stolen in portage out of the men's bags, – about the worst loss they could sustain. And this camp has not yet received the stores which were at Dongola when the base was shifted up here, and the result is that many necessaries of life will have to be gone without. By the time the second half of the Naval Brigade start they will probably have arrived; for their sakes I hope so. Here we have fresh bread, a great boon, but above Hannek we were able to buy a little milk and eggs from time to time, and if one had had a gun no end of wild geese and pigeons might have been shot, but I sent mine back to Halfa. Had I brought it on, I should have had to leave it on the beach here, and it was too good a gun to bring on chance. A good cheap gun would not have mattered, and would have supplied plenty of food. … I have just received such a very nice letter from poor Mrs. Francis Kerr[ii] in answer to mine of condolence. She is, as I knew she would be, quite broken-hearted, but most brave in the way she is bearing up. I never saw a more devoted wife than she was, and a beautiful letter of resignation she wrote, enclosing a mortuary card.

I deeply regret to say a great friend of mine, Colonel ——, who was at our camp for a long time at Abkar, has committed suicide; the last man I should have thought who would have done it, but he had a touch of sunstroke, and went to the hospital at Semneh to be treated, when probably in an insane mind he did the fatal act. He was very much liked, and a more charming companion it has seldom been my lot to come across. … I am so glad to hear the Welds are gone to Ugbrooke; what a charming place! and a truly charming family the Cliffords are, and it is nice for them having Cecily Feilding near them. It is nice for you having your old friend Lady Mostyn so near you: it adds so much to your neighbourhood; but whatever you do, for all our sakes, take the greatest possible care of yourself. I wish you had a better pony to run you about the country, and if I was in England, I would soon present you with a new one.

Oxenham, p. 226/227

The next letter, the last he ever wrote, is dated just four days before the battle of Abu Klea, and was not received till three weeks after all was over. It is written in pencil, but quite legibly. It is given here—with the omission of a short passage of a private nature—just as it stands, without any attempt to correct the abrupt and somewhat elliptical style, which recalls all the more vividly the circumstances under which it was written. Still more noteworthy is the maintenance to the last of the same cheery and buoyant tone which characterizes his letters throughout— 'it is best not to think about' the perils and hardships of that desperate expedition, and 'one soon forgets them'. He still keeps his eye on the scenery, and has plans for future sketches, and remembers that it will interest his mother to hear this; but, on the other hand, he has no illusions; 'few know what the future may bring.' He perfectly understands that 'the whole affair is critical', and – though in writing to his mother he takes care *not* to put that into words – that each successive day may prove to be his last. His brave bright spirit is unbroken, but not from any reckless or timid refusal to look facts in the face; there is as little of foolhardiness as of craven shrinking or distrust.

Letter 18

Rudolph to his Mother, Laura de Lisle

GAKDUL, DESERT OF BAYUDA,
January 13th.

My dearest Mother, – Just a short letter to let you know we have arrived here at the Wells and start to-morrow for Metammeh (Shendy) *en route* to Khartoum.

We came across the desert in four days, and had a pretty hard time of it, about three pints of water a day, and some soldiers had even less. The nights cool, day burning hot, but not to be compared with what it will be later; no time to sketch, all our time taken up looking after our camels and stores. Lost two camels on the way, one dropped down dead; several men knocked down by the sun, but so far we are all well. First night had four hours sleep, started off with moon, 1 a.m., and went on in column till 10 a.m., when we halted for four hours; had no breakfast, and for three days ate only a little biscuit, meat out of the question with so little water. Third day, got to some wells, water thick like liquid mud, and as some of the soldiers had had only one pint of water we forewent (is it English?) ours, so as not to block the way. The sight at Abu Halfa wells one not easily forgotten; men imploring to be allowed a mouthful, and sentries placed near to prevent the crush; but men on the whole retained their discipline. In the desert the difference between before they have their pint of water and afterwards marvellous. If one had had it, one would have given any money for it; a certain number of camels kept on falling out all the way, and some were brought up by rear-guard.

The soldiers wonderfully civil to us, and our men do as well on camels as a great many who expected to see us landed off their backs. Here men and animals had the most delicious water to drink, but to get water for over 1,000 men and 2,500 or perhaps more camels difficult. But now our real difficulties are about to begin, for we shall be cut off from our baggage animals for the whole day, as they are kept to the rear, as we go forward in fighting array, the 'Baggagers' in rear, and we expect a brush or two on the way down, the tribes between here and Metammeh having declared against us, but whether they will show fight remains to be seen. But it will be some time before you get further news from us, for telegraphs don't go across the desert, and except where armed convoys go to the rear to Korti there will be no communication.

We expect to find steamers at Shendy, and if they are – unless stranded over the cataract between that place and Khartoum, and we get through the narrow part of the river lined with the Mahdi's people – we ought to be at Khartoum, with luck, in about a fortnight or less from now. Thirty miles this side of Metammeh a fight is pretty sure to take place. We had 500 men on our flanks trying to get to the wells, but they offered no opposition; two prisoners were, however, taken, wearing the Mahdi's uniform, and some camels with dates, which we have since eaten. We have been here and shall have been two days, and a busy time we have had; got our Gardner Gun mounted, and this morning drilled all our men. The most serious thing is the want of corn for the camels, about eighteen pounds per camel for the whole way.

Bayuda Desert – Standard Bearer, white camel, 14 January 1885. This is one of the last sketches done by Rudolph, taken the day they started out for Metammeh en route to Khartoum.

If we meet with no opposition, Saturday next ought to see us across to the Nile and water again. But I fear the camels, great numbers of them, are in a bad way, but if we can only get them down to the Nile we can get lots of doora [maize] for them, but there is no doubt there will be a good deal of thirst on the way, but it is best not to think about it, and here one soon forgets what one felt on the way here. Some parts of the desert are very pretty, and I think I have in my mind's eye plenty of material for painting; my sketch book has literally fallen to pieces, and I had a fire on my camel which warmed me up pretty well, set on fire by the sun, and several cases of the same occurred to other people, so one was not single even in this. My hands are still pretty bad, but I can hold my sword now if necessary. With the sun burning one's

Camel riding, 14 January 1884.

Notes for future paintings. Rudolph continued to sketch to the end, making rough sketches with notes for when he would work them up into full paintings.

hands all day there is little or no chance of getting them right, and then one's blood must get out of order; no vegetables, and the same corned beef, which on the desert one cannot eat. However, here we have had two good days' food; I mean we were able to eat our rations owing to a good supply of water, but to-night, though in the land of plenty, the men on fatigue are working all night at the wells pumping, etc. Fortunately the Naval Brigade are excused this duty to-night, or this letter could not have been written, and I know what a pleasure it will give you, for we live in the open, and the light we have is a candle surrounded with tin to make a lantern, and one's knee for a table, with a piece of wood across. Had I had time, I would have made a sketch of our men on the march, but an excellent sketch is being sent to the *Graphic* by

Villiers,[i] he having, of course, nothing else to do. Melton Prior,[ii] *Illustrated* artist, is also with us, so my sketches would very likely not be in it. I had neither time not opportunity of sending sketch of the Naval Brigade on the river, with their sails all set and making the best of the passage up.

Lord Wolseley remains at Korti, but he knows what he is about, but there is no use disguising the fact that the whole affair is critical, and it may be one of the greatest successes, or otherwise. If only the Government could have made up their minds six weeks or two months sooner, but no, so we shall have the hot weather to contend with, if the whole programme is carried out and all Gordon's people taken away, but the future only is before us, and few know what it may bring. In the meanwhile we are moving on. Little did I think this time last year I should be where I now am. Lord C. Beresford is with us, and he certainly managed with the General, Sir H. Stewart,[iii] that we should have our fair ration of water. … In this job everything finished is at once forgotten, and the *agony* we went through with those steamers out of mind by this time I expect.[1] My love to all when you write, and tell Freda if she could see me now I should be sent flying out of the doors—four days without washing! and a little bit burnt and dried up generally.[2] I have been wishing I could write to Margaret, but we go on day and night, and have done so by the faintest light of the moon, which, unfortunately, is now finished. With most affectionate love to you, ever, my dearest Mother.

Your very affectionate son,
RUDOLPH DE LISLE.

1. Oxenham – It may be hoped that this is not so. In his official dispatch to the Admiralty, dated Korti, March 16th, 1885, Lord Wosleley says that he "cannot speak too highly of the way in which they [the Naval Brigade] have all done their work, nor too strongly of the value of that work to the Expedition." And more recently, in proposing the toast of the "Navy, Army, and Reserve forces" at the annual dinner of the North London Rifle Club, December 10, 1885, his Lordship is reported in the *Times* of December 11, to have said 'He had himself been brought frequently into contact with the Naval Service, and he could say, and say from his heart, that it had always been a pleasure, and a real pleasure, to do duty with the members of that profession shoulder to shoulder. There had been recent experience of the admirable and glorious manner in which the Navy helped the Army on the Upper Nile during the Egyptian campaign."
2. Oxenham – In his last letter to Lady Howard, dated December 1, 1884, he says 'I hear you are making your house very nice, but that I should expect of you; and if I recollect rightly it is not so very far from the Naval and Military: I wonder how long before one enters that spot again. Some time, I take it.'The same letter evidences the survival to the last of his literary tastes: "What I feel and have felt all along is being unable to have books to read, for we came as 'light' as possible, thinking we were going on in the steamers we hauled through; then those Wolseley boats cropped up, and we were kept back for them." And again, further on: "If you would forward to me some of your papers and magazines which you do not keep, they would be a great boon to the Naval Brigade generally:—*my name*, *Naval Brigade*, *Nile Expedition*, would be sure to reach."

Sketch of Lord Charles Beresford, 16 January 1885. Probably the last sketch Rudolph made before his death the next day at the Battle of Abu Klea.

THE LATE COMMANDER ALFRED PIGOTT, R.N., KILLED IN THE SOUDAN.

THE LATE MAJOR W. H. ATHERTON, 5TH DRAGOON GUARDS, KILLED IN THE SOUDAN.

THE LATE LIEUT. RUDOLPH DE LISLE, R.N., KILLED IN THE SOUDAN.

THE LATE LIEUTENANT RUDOLPH DE LISLE, R.N.

Among the officers accompanying Brigadier-General Sir Herbert Stewart's force across the Desert, in the advance from Korti to Metammeh, who fell in the battle of Abou Klea, on Saturday, the 17th inst., we regret to learn the death of Lieutenant Rudolph De Lisle, to whose pencil this Journal was indebted for some excellent Sketches of the cataracts of the Upper Nile, and of the difficult operations performed in getting the steam-boats and rowing-boats to pass up from Wady Halfa to Dongola. Lieutenant Rudolph Edward Lisle March-Phillipps De Lisle was the eighth son of the late Ambrose March-Phillipps De Lisle, of Garendon Park and Grâcedieu Manor, Leicestershire, and of his wife, Laura Clifford, eldest daughter of Thomas, the fourth son of Hugh, fourth Lord Clifford, of Chudleigh. He was born at Grâce-dieu Manor on Nov. 23, 1851. After a year at Oscott College, he went to Gosport, to the late Mr. Burney, to be prepared for the naval cadets' training-ship, Britannia. He there took a first class on leaving. In May, 1869, he joined H.M.S. Cadmus for his first voyage. He was in H.M.S. Liverpool when the first flying squadron went round the world, returning to England in 1871. He was in H.M.S. Cameleon at the time of the war between Peru and Chili, and, for his gallant conduct at the time of the burning of Lima, he was made an honorary member of the Fire Brigade. He was promoted to be Sub-Lieutenant in March, 1873, and Lieutenant in May, 1877. He left H.M.S. Alexandra, in August last year, to join Commodore Hammill for the Nile Expedition, where he distinguished himself by his great energy and activity; and he was regarded as an officer of high promise, whose death is a loss to the naval service.

The *Freemason* states that the Prince of Wales has appointed Brother T. W. Tew, Provincial Grand Master of West Yorkshire, and Brother Sir Hedworth Williamson, Provincial Grand Master for Durham.

THE LATE COMMANDER A. PIGOTT, R.N.

One of the naval officers engaged in the Nile Expedition, whose services were of great value in managing the ascent of the rapids or cataracts by the flotilla of whale-boats and other vessels, conveying soldiers and stores, was Commander Alfred Pigott, previously in command of the store-ship Humber, in the Red Sea. This able and gallant officer led the First Division of the Naval Brigade, under Lord Charles Beresford, attached to General Sir Herbert Stewart's advanced force in its march across the Desert from Korti, and we regret to find his name among those killed on the 17th inst., in the conflict at the Wells of Abou Klea. He entered the Royal Navy in 1861, and served in her Majesty's ships Queen, Marlborough, Mutine, Inconstant, Lord Warden, and Hercules. He became Sub-Lieutenant in December, 1867, and Lieutenant in February, 1872. In June, 1877, he was selected to be Second Lieutenant on board H.M.S. Britannia, naval cadets' training-ship, during the training of Prince Albert Victor Edward of Wales and Prince George of Wales.

Obituary of Rudolph De Lisle, Commander Pigott and Major Atherton, *Illustrated London News*, 31 January 1885.

Other Letters

Letter 19

Rudolph, aged 7, to his mother, Laura de Lisle

Gracedieu Manor
11 Juin 1860

Ma chére Maman

Jai été bien content d'apprendre que ma bonne petite Marie[i] allait maintenant un peu mieux, nous avons tous été trés fachés de savoir qu'elle avait été si malade. François[ii] a reçu hier votre letter, il vous en remercie beaucoup, nous avons tous beaucoup aimé ce que vous nous dites de la procession, j'aurais bien voulu être avec vous je vous assure. J'aimerais tant voir mes bonnes petites sœurs, et être prés de la mer, cela est si amusant et si joli. Depuis que vous êtes á Londres, je n'ai pas encore pu aller a cheval, j'en suis trés fâché, il fait toujours si mauvais temps, j'éspére que ce sera pour aujourd hui car il fait un peu de soleil. Le bois est maintenant trés joli tout est en fleurs, notre jardin aussi est magnifique, seulement nous voudrions bien qu'il y eut une allée coupée dans le champ pour y aller, car l'herbe commence á être trés haute.

Je suis bien content, Melle [iii] m'a promis de me montrer á faire des soustractions cette semaine. Comme c'est aujourd'hui le jour de naissance de François[iv] nous avons un demi-congé et notre thé dans les petites tasses.

Je vous envoie bien des baisers, et aussi á Papa, Alice[v] et Freda.[vi]

Votre fils affect.[ne]
Rudolph Lisle Phillipps.

TRANSLATION

Gracedieu Manor
11 June 1860

My dear Mother

I was so happy to learn that my good little Mary[i] was a little better. We were all very annoyed to know that she has been very ill. Francis[ii] received yesterday your letter; he thanks you very much for it. We have all very much liked what you have told us as to the procession; I would very much have liked to be with you, I can assure you. I would love to see my dear little sisters and be near the sea as it is so amusing and pretty. Since you have been in London, I have not been able to ride and I am very annoyed, but the weather is always so bad. I hope it will happen today as it is a little sunny. The woods are very pretty and all in flower; our garden is also magnificent but we would like a path cut through the field to get there as the grass is beginning to be very high.

I am very happy Mademoiselle[iii] has promised to show me how to subtract this week. As today is the birthday of Francis,[iv] we have a half day holiday and take our tea in the small cups.

I send you many kisses and also to Papa, Alice[v] and Freda.[vi]

Your very affectionate son
Rudolph Lisle Phillipps.

Letter 20

Rudolph, aged 11, To His Cousin, Captain (later Admiral) Ryder

LONGCLIFFE LODGE, LOUGHBRO,
June 12*th*, 1864

MY DEAR COUSIN ALFRED,

I hope that you will not mind my writing you a letter. I am tremendously anxious to become a sailor. And I want to know everything concerning ships, and the sea. So if you would be so kind as to write a letter and explain everything to do with the naval profession and all about it, should be much obliged. I only wish to-morrow was the day for me to enter the Navy. The days seem years to me. I wish I was on board a ship this moment, but above all ships in the world I would sooner be in your ship. If I was in the same ship as you I should not mind being sent up to the masthead for a punishment. I should like to be in a battle on sea very much indeed. I like rowing immensely. I wish you were here for me to ask you millions of questions all about everything. I should very much like to know the name of the ship you command, and if it is a very nice one. I intend to be a very brave sailor, and like Everard to get the Victoria Cross, if I can.

We have got a very nice book giving an account of the principal people who got the Victoria Cross, and I am very fond of reading it. I have got some more sea-books, *The Three Midshipmen*[i] – it is a first–rate book – also *Masterman Ready*,[ii] which is a capital book: perhaps you have read it. I think I have read *Robinson Crusoe*[iii] through a dozen times, as also the *Life of Lord Nelson*,[iv] and I rather think I shall get *The Child of the Atlantic Ocean*,[v] and *The British Seaman*.[vi] Can you recommend me any more sea-books? Also I have got *The Little Savage*.[1, vii]

And have you got a monkey on board your ship, and does it play any fine tricks? We had three or four good rows in our pond at Gracedieu, though we got our feet nicely wet, because the boat leaked a great deal; in some places it leaked about two inches deep. Will you please tell me, if you write, any little adventure which happened to you in a storm, and how the sailors managed the ship? It is quite decided that Frank[viii] is going to New Zealand, and I am to be a sailor.

Good-bye, my dear Cousin Alfred; hoping to hear from you soon,

I remain,

Your affectionate Cousin,

RUDOLPH DE LISLE

1. Oxenham – It may be mentioned that birthday presents in his family had always taken the shape of books. And Rudolph's taste for reading led him very early to add to his store by subscribing for Cassell's illustrated historical works. He and his brother Edwin were also fond of printing with a little printing-machine they had at Gracedieu, and some specimens of their work are still preserved.

Letter 21

Laura de Lisle to her son, Rudolph

Chideock Warren[i]
Sep.r – 7 – 1884

Darling Rudolph

You may be sure that I read with the greatest avidity the daily reports of the goings on in Egypt especially on the Nile. I was very sorry to see in the *Standard* that last Thursday the expedition under Col. Hammil[ii] had not succeeded as he had hope in bringing the Steamer over the Cataract. I suppose that you were engaged there[iii] – but the *Standard* went on to say that it was all owing to the low state of the Nile that the attempt had not succeeded. One thing I know is that if it had depended on your exertions alone it would have done so – I see the Nile in yesterday's paper is said "to be rising". I sincerely hope it may continue to do so as that is what you will like. Sep.r 10. I have not had time to finish my letter before today. I see in *The Times* of the 9th that the Nile has fallen 6 inches & that the ——— of Dongola[iv] says 'it will not rise again'. What a pity Col. Hammil was not attended to when he wanted to pass the Cataracts 3 weeks ago. But our present government well deserves the name of 'never ready'. I need hardly add how much I hope & pray for your future success & that it may be rewarded by promotion.

I wrote to you last Sep.r 3. There is not much to tell you since. I thanked you for your letter of August 19 which I sent same day to Alice. Margaret &c had read it at Onebarrow before sending it on to me as they were so anxious to know how you were getting on. As Mena & the older girls left the 'Warren' on Monday for Spetchleyv to attend the Worcester Musical Festival I came here as Charles & Mary Weld[vi] had wished me to pay them a visit before leaving this neighbourhood. I find them very much altered. He is so very infirm on his legs, & altogether 'quite an old man' tho' a year & a half younger than I am. The decorations of his lovely church[vii] he never will finish now. But he has done the principal parts. The dome 3 altars and what remains he wishes Chrissy and Cicely[viii] to do. Nothing can be nicer than his manners to all Mina's children of whom he is justly proud, as also of their admirable father.

Fred turned up yesterday afternoon. He had left Beaufort Castle Monday & found trains fitted in better than he had calculated so arrived to our just surprise before 4 instead of about 8. He is gone today to shoot birds. I suppose Everard is trying his hand at them at Garendon this week. Margaret wrote me how he was expected back last Saturday. Mena & her girls return tomorrow, for dinner so I shall do the same. I go to Alice either on Saturday or Monday for 10 days or so. Freda has left her again & is gone to Freshwater, Isle of Wight for sea bathing till she takes possession of her house 19 Cadogan Sq.re, Ocr 6. She wants Margaret to help her to furnish it and as Bernard goes to Cambridge Ocr 4, she will be at liberty.

Have I told you that my dear wise friend D.r Ullathorne[ix] told me he was pleased to hear that Bern. was going to Cambridge & not to Oxford because there is much less infidelity there, & Canon McMullen[x] who has been staying here told me that Card. Newman was also of that opinion & thought it much safer for Catholics to go to C. than Oxford. So I am very pleased. Edwin I believe is at Wardour.[xi] I wish all them visiting would lead to some good result & get him a nice Catholic wife with some money but I am afraid this latter temporal blessing is not to be the fate of our family. But we have others in exchange in health & strength & without those no wealth can be enjoyed.

Canon MacMullen preached us a beautiful sermon on the Providence of God', taking the Gospel of the Sunday for his text. I wish you had heard it. He has a wonderful knowledge of the H. Scriptures, & he quoted all my favourite texts which have been of such wonderful support to me in the hours of my great trials. He particularly dwelt on the one chosen by Cardinal Manning[xii] as his text for his sermon on the death of the Prince Imperial[xiii] "What I do now thou knowest not but shalt know hereafter" I sent you a copy of that beautiful & most instructive sermon (at the time) which I almost know by heart having read it so often to the poor people when they too had lost dear ones. Conformity to God's holy will has always since quite a child been my favourite virtue and the more one can practice it, the easier ones path thro' life becomes, for we feel the hand of a loving Father in all that happens, & that one day we shall see that all He ordains will work for good in those who love Him.

I hope that you are very particular in trying to have great purity of intention in all you do, for remember the great merit that the most trivial actions (& you are called up on to do great ones) will lay up for us provided united to the merits of our Saviour's passion & death. I am so glad you have M.r Pollen in your company & I see that the 500 Canadians that are going to Egypt have a Priest[xiv] coming with them.

The Harvest I fancy must be nearly over in Leicestershire. Margaret wrote word that Gerard would finish his, last Saturday weather permitting. Here we had torrents of rain all day long I hope it was not so at Onebarrow.

I am sure you will be sorry to hear that Mary Ann has given me notice to leave. She said the household was so very different to what it was for the first year & more, to which I quite agree, & with much crying she announced she must go. Frida is going to have her. I am very glad to have found such a good comfortable place for her, for she truly deserves it. For a better servant never has entered a gentleman's house. Also Mary Ann did not like our French Cook so well as she like <S.A. Peach?> (left to marry) nor my french maid so well as Emma Wale who had to leave on account of bad health. But it is a great nuisance losing an old servant & having to look out for a new one.

M.r Weld is going to take me a drive to Bridport for the letters, 2d delivery so I must end herein with wishing you all possible blessings and that you will be < > to me, & come out of this war? with every sort of honour & glory. Believe me to be very darling Rudolph

Ever your most aff.ate Mother

Laura de Lisle

I hope you will write when you can, if only half a sheet of paper & written in pencil. When that is the case please to write with large letters.

Letter 22

Laura de Lisle to her son, Rudolph

October 30. 1884
Onebarrow Lodge
Loughborough

Darling Rudolph

The *Illustrated London News* of Oc^{r} 25 has for its first picture 'a critical Moment'.[i] It is taken just when your boat was apart and there are 2 figures clinging to the ropes to get into the Nassif Kheir. One or 2 more figures are standing on the upset boat, & one of them I imagine must be <u>you</u> because I know you would always think of the safety of others before your own, & see your companions <landed?> into the steamer before you would attempt to get into it. *The Times* on Oc^{r} 16th has a most interesting article 'the Nile Expedition' and it was there we read the account of your escape & that of your companions in the boat. I need hardly add I have carefully cut out the article to paste it in a scrapbook. Your last letter was dated Sepr 26. It is a comfort to know from day to day that you are safe, for all casualties are named in the Telegrams. You may imagine how eagerly I read them as soon as the papers are brought in. You are sure of getting my letters now because I am sending them thro' the Admiralty every week. Mr. Hubert Dormer proposed to me to do so. & I was very glad to accept his kind proposal. I think I have no news to tell you since my last letter of this day went 23. Gwendaline has since sent me the inclosed beautiful prayer which she has printed for you. I am particularly fond of it, I say it daily, & so does Mena. I advise you to do the same. We cannot be too ready for whatever Alm. God has in store for us & we know that whatever He sends is always in love, even when He punishes.

You will be glad to hear that Dr Morgan[ii] the head Master of Jesus Coll. Cambridge has sent a very satisfactory report of Bernard to his late Crammer, Mr Hepworth[iii] of Sheps^{d} Dr M. says 'he is well impressed with B. who attends lectures &c very regularly and that he considers his University career will be a decided benefit to him'. I sent the copys I took to Margaret who is still in London with Frida 19 Cadogan Square, S.W. and asked her to return it, but of course she has forgotten to do so. I hope she won't lose it as I shall like to keep it at least for the present.

Everard is certainly a most active landlord. He rides about daily on Bob and yesterday found on 2 farms one was Peberdy at Holywell, the outlets of the drains he had himself put in during this last spring, stopped up! Another year or two these two farms would require draining and this is the way things have been neglected by unprincipled tenants who don't take the least care of the land, only get off all they can, & put nothing on.

I hear from Edwin that he will be here this afternoon so his (the former lumber room) is getting ready for him. He has the prospect of a good literary Employment to begin in Jany. I only hope it will not be another bubble like all his other schemes have been. He is very much to be pitied and he has always been so very economical, never got into a penny of debt that he really deserves a better fate. I am always hoping something will turn up to his advantage, & hitherto I have always been disappointed.

Lt. Poore RN and Coki and 'A Critical Moment'. The original of 'A Critical Moment' was lost. For Rudolph's original sketches of Lt. Poore RN and Coki, see page 79.

The Frank Eystons[iv] have been away since the middle of September & are not expected before the 15 Nov. They are now staying with his Parents. He is a very good shot so he gets invited to shoot in the neighbourhood & Angela is very popular. I am sorry to say the Edward Wolseleys[v] leave this week. They have taken a house at Hendon till their own, which they are building at Weybridge, is ready for them. His business takes him so continually to London that he wished to be nearer. Angela will miss her dreadfully as they met most days.

Most probably the dow.[r] Lady Mostyn[vi] (Lord Lovat's[vii] sister) will take Charnwood Lodge. She is negotiating about it. She is a most charming person. We once staid 10 days at Talacre[viii] & she & I became great friends. That was very many years ago as Alice & Frida were with us, and we have not met since. I fancy we shall not recognize each other. We must both be so very much altered. She has one unmarried daughter[ix] who lives with her. I hope that she & Margaret will be friends. Gerard was at Oscott with 3 of her sons, but his favourite, Frank,[x] is ordained a Priest just lately, & another lives in London. He is in business, a third lives with his mother – so Gerard will find him pleasant – tho' I suspect Sunday will be the only day he will be able to spend time to Amuse himself – & then the amusement consists generally in walking over to Garendon to inspect the animals he has got there. I am glad to say he has got rid of nearly half (400) sheep he brought with him from Scotland His own herding (Shropshires) are greatly sought after. 2 men came to buy some from some distance. Unluckily he was gone to a sale at Leicester whence he bought back 4 foals. And his shepherd told him G would not sell them for 4£ a piece. But G regrets he did not see them as he probably would have made a good bargain.

I am glad to say my little pony is quite well again. She took me to Mass last Saturday for the first time since I returned from Chideock & Bournemouth in September. She goes capitally now she is clipped & I hope she will last me some time yet. That same day ~~Everard~~ Gerard went to shoot at the Outwoods. M.r Ellis, Cap.n Heygate & M.r Johnstone[xi] were the other 3 guns. They killed 58 Head. M.r Herrick is so very kind in asking Gerard for he is not a good shot. He has never had the practicing that the rest of you have had.

Our female establishment is entirely new since you were here. I think I told you at the time that <S.A. Peach?> left to marry a brick layer much against her family's wishes for they looked higher for her. But she is very happy & that is the principal & after all I doubt she & he made a mesalliance – <S.A. Concannon?> who used to come & help formerly (a widow twice) has succeeded Peach. I have Emma a French girl, Alice's cast off goods, as my maid & another called Mary Stibbings as Mary's Ann's successor. New brooms always sweep well, & she does her work extremely well. She has been here 5 weeks, and Mary Ann is gone to Frida when she has a half girl to help her at present we are no loser by the exchange. Every thing is cleared off, lamps put out & Maids gone to bed at 10. The tea things are of course left in the drawing room as well as lamp Gerard always goes to bed at 10 & so do I. I wish that Everard could follow our good example but he always will stay up till after 11. That is his time for reading, at present it is the life of that glorious Gordon[xii] which I bought at a Railway Station & it is most interesting – a real hero of tomorrow he is. But our government, it appears to me have behaved shamefully in not responding earlier to his demands for help. I see your friend Major Trotter[xiii] has been decorated by the Khetive & I see her Majesty has allowed it. I think I have told you he is Dow.r Lady Belper's nephew.

Gerard & Everard send you their love. Take great care of yourself my darling Rudolph & May Heaven protect you & bring you safe home after all the perils that surround you at the moment. Believe me ever to be

Your most aff Mother

Laura de Lisle

Letter 23

Lord (later Admiral) Charles Beresford, Commander, Naval Brigade, to Laura de Lisle

This letter was written in pencil and sent to H.M.S. *Alexandra* 'To be forwarded'. It was received by Laura on 7 May 1885.

Korti
Soudan
March 9. 1885.

Madam

Please allow me to assure you how heartily & sincerely I sympathise with you in the sad loss of your gallant Son; to know him was to love and respect him. He was one of the very best Officers I have ever met in the Service. So Smart, So cheery, So energetic and So kind hearted. He was the life and Soul of our little Brigade. No work was too much for him and no duty too long for him, & he was always cheery at the end of it. Your loss is too Sad to think of. What mine is – I have lost a gallant, true & noble friend. The Service has lost one of its best and brightest Officers – Your Son must have been carried away in the first violent rush of the Arabs in which all the men working the Gun were killed or wounded, excepting one man & myself who were knocked down & so miraculously escaped. I found him after the battle about 20 yards to the left rear of the Gun, having evidently fought till the last.[i] A few paces from him was his friend & Messmate Com.[r] Pigott. The Officers & men of the Brigade were deeply grieved at the loss of your gallant Son, as he was beloved by them all from his splendid character & kindly dispositions.

Again assuring you of my heartfelt sympathy for you in your sad loss,

I am Madam
Yours very faithfully

Signed Charles Beresford
Commanding Naval Brigade

Notes

Letter 1: 15 August 1884 – H.M.S. Alexandra, off Alexandria

i Probably Admiral of the Fleet Sir Alfred Phillipps Ryder KCB (1820–1888), Rudolph's first cousin, once removed.

ii Lieutenant General The Honourable Sir James Charlemagne Dormer (1834–1893), appointed Chief of Staff of the army of occupation in Egypt in 1882.

iii Francis Gabriel Hungerford Pollen RN (1862–1944). Appointed Commander, Order of the British Empire (CBE) in 1919.

iv Tynte Ford Hammill, RN (1851–1894). Promoted to Captain 1885 for his service with the Nile Expeditionary Force. 1892 appointed Companion in the Military Division of the Order of the Bath (CB).

Letter 2: 19 August 1884 – S.S. Benhah, off Keneh

i Captain Arthur William May (1854–1925), surgeon on HMS *Alexandra*. Later Sir Arthur William May, KCB, FRCS, Surgeon Vice Admiral, RN (ret.); late Medical Director General, Medical Department of the Navy, Honorary Physician to the King.

ii In the 1881 Childers Reform, the 46th (South Devonshire) Regiment of Foot was merged with the 32nd (Cornwall Light Infantry) Regiment of Foot to form the Duke of Cornwall's Light Infantry, the 32nd forming the 1st Battalion and the 46th the 2nd Battalion of the new Regiment.

iii In the 1881 Childers Reform, the 42nd (Royal Highland) Regiment of Foot (The Black Watch) was merged with the 73rd (Perthshire) Regiment of Foot to form The Black Watch (Royal Highlanders), the 42nd forming the 1st Battalion and the 73rd the 2nd Battalion of the new Regiment.

iv It is possible that Oxenham has this wrong, and the General referred to is General Sir Frederick Charles Arthur Stephenson, GCB (1821–1911) who was appointed Commander-in-chief of the British Army of Occupation in Cairo in 1883. There was a Nicholson, who ended his career as a Field-Marshal, but who was at this point in time merely a Brevet Major, serving with the Indian contingent of the Egyptian campaign.

v By special permission of King Edward VII, the Victoria Cross was presented to Edwin de Lisle (1852–1920), Everard's only surviving brother, and it is now cherished by the family.

Letter 3: 25 August 1884 – P.S. Ghizeh near Wady Halfa, Upper Nile

i First Lieutenant Alfred Pigott (1847–1885). Made a Commander just two weeks before his death at the Battle of Abu Klea.

ii Major-General The Honourable Edward James Montagu-Stuart-Wortley (1857–1934).

iii Horatio Herbert Kitchener, 1st Earl Kitchener KG, KP, GCB, OM, GCSI, GCMG, GCIE, PC (1850–1916).

iv Possibly Lt. William C. Reid, formerly of HMS *Monarch*.

v In the 1881 Childers Reform, the 35th Royal Sussex Regiment of Foot was merged with the 107th Regiment of Foot (Bengal Light Infantry) Regiment of Foot, together with the Royal Sussex Light Infantry Militia and the Cinque Ports and Sussex units of the Volunteer force to form the Royal Sussex Regiment, the 35th forming the 1st Battalion of the new Regiment.

vi Muhammad Ahmad bin Abd Allah (1844–1885), Sufi religious leader of the Samaniyya order in Sudan.

vii Probably Major George Robert James Shakespear (1842–1926), Bengal Service Corps. In 1881, re–assigned to staff duties in preparation for active service in the Sudan. 15 June 1885 appointed a Brevet Lieutenant Colonel, serving in the Sudan as the Director of Transport. 26 August 1885 *The Times* published Lord Wolseley's despatch from Cairo to the Secretary of State for War where he indicates that Shakespear was '*deserving of special mention for his service in the Sudan while performing his duties as the Senior Transport Officer, Assistant Commissary General, Transport Branch*.' Also awarded the Egypt Medal 1882 with clasp [SUAKIN 1885] and Khedive's Star for his service during the Sudan campaign of 1885.

Letter 4: 8 September 1884 – Camp of the Naval Brigade, Abkar

i Lieutenant Colonel Sir Henry Trotter, KCMG, CB (1841–1919).

Letter 5: 18 September 1884 – Naval Camp, Abkar, Nubia, 2nd Cataract

i The Navy List of June 1884 does not list 'Woodcock' amongst the complement of HMS *Monarch*.

ii Unable to identify. Most likely a blue-jacket, whose names were not included in The Navy List.

iii His sister, Alice (1840–1926), widow of The Honourable Arthur Strutt (1842–1877).

iv Hon. Cecilia Mary Clifford (1860–1919), daughter of Charles Hugh Clifford, 8th Baron Clifford of Chudleigh and Hon. Agnes Catherine Louisa Petre (1826–1891), who married Rudolph Robert Basil Aloysius Augustine Feilding, 9th Earl of Denbigh, on 24 September 1884

v The Dowager Lady Clifford, née The Hon. Agnes Catherine Louisa Petre (1826–1891), widow of Charles Hugh Clifford, 8th Baron Clifford of Chudleigh (1819–1880).

vi Body of sailors serving in a ground combat role to augment land forces.

vii Field Marshal Garnet Joseph Wolseley, 1st Viscount Wolseley, KP, GCB, OM, GCMG, VD, PC (1833–1913), Commander of the Nile Expedition.

viii His sister, Margaret Mary (1855–1895) who in 1886 became a Franciscan Sister of the 3rd Order Regular, dying at Mill Hill Convent, London, in 1895.

ix His brother, Gerard (1860–1924), attended Cirencester Agricultural College 1878–1880, later moving to Saskatchewan to farm.

x Admiral of the Fleet Lord John Hay, GCB (1827–1916), Royal Navy officer and politician; Rudolph served under him on HMS *Alexandra*.

Letter 6: 26 September 1884 – Naval Camp, Abkar, Nubia

i Robert Archibald James Montgomerie (1855–1908). At this time serving as a Lieutenant on HMS *Invincible*. He later rose to the rank of Rear Admiral, CB, CMG, and CVO. 1877 received the Albert Medal (the precursor of the George Medal) for Lifesaving.

ii A naval rating, i.e. a junior enlisted officer who is neither a warrant officer or commissioned officer.

Letter 7: 22 October 1884 – Naval Camp, Abkar, Nubia

i Wolseley selected modified Royal Navy whalers, approximately 33ft long, 6ft 7in wide and 2ft 6in deep, with twelve oars, two masts and a removable rudder. The boats had the capacity for a dozen men plus 100 day's supplies.

ii His nephews, Everard (1862–1947) and Bernard (1864–1921).

Letter 8: 25 October 1884 – Abkar

i Mary Lyall Hillyar, née Taylor (1788–1884), widow of Admiral Sir James Hillyar KCB KCH (1769–1843).

Letter 9: 1 November 1884 – Camp of the Naval Brigade, Sarras

i The *voyageurs*: French Canadian and First Nations boatmen skilled in the transport of goods via river recruited by Wolseley, who had encountered them during his expedition down the Red River to Fort Garry in 1869–1870 to suppress the Red River Rebellion. 386 were recruited on a 6-month contract, arriving at Wadi Halfa October 26, 1884.

ii Charles William de la Poer Beresford, 1st Baron Beresford, GCB, GCVO, FRSGS (1846–1919), styled Lord Charles Beresford between 1859 and 1916, British admiral and Member of Parliament.

iii His brother, Edwin Joseph Lisle March Phillipps de Lisle MP (1852–1920).

iv In the 1881 Childers Reform, the 38th Staffordshire Regiment of Foot was merged with the 80th Regiment of Foot (Staffordshire Volunteers) to form the South Staffordshire Regiment, the 38th forming the 1st Battalion of the new Regiment.

v His sister, Alice Mary Elizabeth March Phillipps de Lisle (1840–1926), Mrs Arthur Strutt.

Letter 10: 10 November 1884 – Naval Camp, Sarras

i Sub-Lieutenant Colin Richard Keppel (1862–1947), later Admiral Sir Colin Richard Keppel, GCVO, KCIE, CB, DSO.

ii Lieutenant George William Tyler (1852–1933), assigned to service on Picket Boats on the Nile, August 1884.

iii A light boat carried aboard merchant and war vessels to serve as a tender.

iv Colonel William Francis Butler, later Lieutenant General Sir William Francis Butler GCB, PC (Ire) (1838–1910), British Army officer, writer, and adventurer.

Letter 11: 20 November 1884 – Naval Camp, Gemai

i Osman Digna (c.1840–1926); a follower of Muhammad Ahmad, becoming his best-known military commander during the Mahdist War.

ii Captain Harry Holdsworth Rawson RN, Captain on HMS *Alexandra*. Later Admiral Sir Harry Holdsworth Rawson GCB, GCMG (1843–1910), leader of the Benin Expedition of 1897, looting and burning the palace, and confiscating a large number of the Benin Bronzes and other royal treasures.

iii Lieutenant Richard Poore of HMS *Invincible*, later Admiral Sir Richard Poore, 4th Baronet KCB, CVO, JP, DL (1853–1930).

iv 110 acres of ancient woodland to the south of Loughborough; one of the oldest surviving woodland sites in Charnwood, Leicestershire.

Letter 12: 30 November 1884 – Naval Camp, Gemai

i Experienced fishermen from the Kroo or Kru tribe in Sotta Krou, in what is now Liberia in West Africa.

ii Arthur Bouchard (1845–1896), French-Canadian priest and missionary in Khartoum 1879–1881. In September 1884 Bouchard returned to the Sudan as chaplain to a contingent of *voyageurs*.

iii Probably John Windham, Naval Cadet May 1867–July 1869 on HMS *Britannia*, *Victory*, *Bristol*, *Bellerophon*, *Revenge* and *Royal Alfred*. Midshipman on HMS *Royal Alfred* July 1869–October 1873, at which point he was discharged for 'repeated misconduct', which would certainly fit in with Rudolph's description of him having had a 'chequered career'.

iv Christopher Bethel (1856–1884). His murder while attempting to drive Boer mercenaries off Baralong land on July 31, 1884 triggered British intervention in what was to become British Bechuanaland.

v Hon. Cecilia Mary Clifford (1860–1919), daughter of Charles Hugh Clifford, 8th Baron Clifford of Chudleigh and Hon. Agnes Catherine Louisa Petre, who married Rudolph Robert Basil Aloysius Augustine Feilding, 9th Earl of Denbigh, on 24 September 1884.

vi His sister, Winifred Mary (1841–1909), wife of Rt. Hon. Lord Edward George FitzAlan-Howard, 1st Baron Howard of Glossop (1818–1883).

Letter 13: 6 December 1884 – Naval Camp, Gemai

i Admiral Frederick Ross Boardman RN, CB (1843–1927). Promoted to Captain 1882. Per his Service Record, 16 September, 1884, 'in command of whole of Navy of Nile during Khartoum Expedition (excepting Naval Brigade)'.

ii In the 1881 Childers Reform, the 75th Stirlingshire Regiment of Foot was merged with the 92nd (Gordon Highlanders) Regiment of Foot to form the Gordon Highlanders, the 75th forming the 1st Battalion of the new Regiment.

iii The 18th (Royal Irish) Regiment of Foot was not particularly affected by the 1881 Childers Reforms as it already comprised of 2 battalions and thus there was no need to amalgamate with a second regiment. The Regiment was, however, renamed, becoming the Royal Irish Regiment.

iv In the 1881 Childers Reform, the 79th (Queen's Own Cameron Highlanders) Regiment of Foot was redesignated as the 1st Battalion Queen's Own Cameron Highlanders.

v Colonel Coleridge Grove (1839–1920), later Major-General Sir Coleridge Grove KCB.

vi Night Blindness (Nyctalopia), an inability to see well at night or in poor light.

Letter 14: 14 December 1884 – Naval Brigade Camp, Ambigol

i Sub-Lt. Edward Lionel Munro RN (1862–1920), second son of Sir Campbell Munro of Lindertis, 3rd Bt. 1887 changed his name to Edward Lionel Walker-Munro by Royal Licence on his marriage to Mabel Zoe Walker (1866–1934), heiress to the Eastwood Colliery fortune.

ii James John Webber (1863–1952). Retired with the rank of Lieutenant 1917, was promoted to Lieutenant Commander in 1925.

iii Unable to identify. Blue-jackets were not individually named in the Navy Lists.

Letter 15: 20 December 1884 – Sarkamatto, above Dal

i His sister, Philomena (1836–1903), married 1859 Sir Frederick Aloysius Weld GCMG (1823–1891); 13 children.

ii His sister, Gwendoline (1845–1914), who had entered an order of Benedictine of nuns in 1869.

iii His sister, Margaret (1855–1895), who was to enter an order of Franciscan nuns in 1886.

Letter 16: 1 January 1885 – Naval Brigade, 70 miles above Dongola

i Grace's Guide to British Industrial History has two advertisements for this company (one 1887, one 1894), locating them in Vyse Street, Birmingham, in which they offer an illustrated catalogue containing over a 1,000 copper-plate engravings of watches at wholesale prices. Any watch purchased from the catalogue, on receipt of a cheque in payment, would be sent free in the United Kingdom and anywhere in the 'Postal World' for 2s 6d.

Letter 17: 6 January 1885 – Korti

i Colonel John Donald Hamill Stewart, CMG (1845–1884), accompanied General Gordon to Khartoum in 1884 as his assistant. Wounded during the siege, Stewart led an attempt to break the blockade aboard the Steamer *Abbas* in September 1884, along with the British consul Frank Power, the French consul Léon Herbin, and some other residents of Khartoum. The *Abbas* ran aground on a rock near Abu Hamad, where all passengers and crew were killed by Arab tribes ashore.

ii Francis Ernest Kerr (1840–1884), son of Reverend Lord Henry Francis Charles Kerr (1800–1882) and Louisa Dorothea Hope (1811–1884), married 1870 Mary Frances, née Monteith (d. 1916), 10 children.

Letter 18: 13 January 1885 – Gakdul, Desert of Bayuda

i Frederic Villiers (1851–1922), British war artist and war correspondent.

ii Melton Prior (1845–1910), English artist and war correspondent for *The Illustrated London News* from the early 1870s until 1904.

iii Major-General Sir Herbert Stewart KCB ADC (1843–1885). Entrusted with the command of the column sent across the Metemma desert, on 17 January 1885, they met the enemy near the wells of Abu Klea, the battle in which Rudolph lost his life. On the morning of the 19th, Stewart was wounded and was forced to hand over command. He died a month later from his wounds and was buried at Jakdul.

Letter 19: 11 June 1860 – Rudolph, aged 7, to his Mother, Laura de Lisle

i Mary (1843–1860). Unfortunately, Mary was to die of consumption on 8 October 1860. In her diary entry for 5 June 1860, Laura notes that Mary is coughing up blood during her stay at St Leonards.

ii Francis 'Frank' (1851–1883), Rudolph's older brother by two years.

iii Governess to the younger children 1854–1860. Not named.

iv Born 11 June 1851 at Grace Dieu.

v Alice (1840–1926), later Mrs Arthur Strutt.

vi Winifred (1841–1909), later Lady Howard of Glossop.

Letter 20: 12 June 1864 – Rudolph, aged 11, to Captain (later Admiral) Alfred Ryder

i *The Three Midshipmen* by W.H.G. Kingston (1815–1880), English writer of boys' adventure novels. Tells the story of three young boys who meet at boarding school and then join the navy. Their stories are carried on in *The Three Lieutenants*, *The Three Commanders*, and, finally, *The Three Admirals*.

ii *Masterman Ready, or the Wreck of the Pacific* by Captain Frederick Marryat (1792–1848), a story of the adventures of the Seagrave family who are shipwrecked at sea, and survive on a desert island with the assistance of veteran sailor, Masterman Ready.

iii *Robinson Crusoe* by Daniel Defoe (c. 1660–1731), the story of a castaway who spends 28 years on a remote tropical island.

iv Probably *The Life of Lord Nelson* by Robert Southey (1774–1843), Poet Laureate (1813–1843), critic, historian, and reviewer. Southey greatly admired Nelson, and his biography published in 1813 was one of his most popular works.

v Unable to identify; it is possible Rudolph has mistaken the title of the book.

vi Probably *Britain's Bulwarks; Or The British Seaman: A Poem in Eight Books* by George Woodley (1786–1846), first published in 1811. In later life a poet, newspaper editor, inventor, cleric and missionary, when young he served on a British man-of-war, and reportedly was writing verse for the amusement of his fellow sailors by the time he was 12.

vii *The Little Savage* by Frederick Marryat (1792–1848). Completed by his son Francis Samuel Marryat (1826–1885), and published in 1848 after Frederick Marryat's death, it tells the story of a young boy stranded on an uninhabited island with his father's murderer.

viii Frank went, instead, to Western Australia, where he died of a heart attack a few months after his marriage.

Letter 21: 7 September 1884 – Laura de Lisle to Rudolph

i The parish of Chideock, Dorset lies between Bridport to the west and Charmouth to the east. Chideock Manor was built in 1811 by the Weld family.

ii Confusingly, there were two Hammills in the Nile Expeditionary Force. Commander Tynte Ford Hammill RN (1851–1894) and Colonel Denzil Hammill (1840–1891) of the 1st Gordon Highlanders. They do not appear to have been related. The newspapers of the date were reporting on both Commander and Colonel Hammill's efforts to get a steamer over the Cataract. However, the report in the *London Evening Standard*, 6 September 1884, p.3, makes it clear that in this case Laura is talking about Col. Hammill of the Gordon Highlanders.

iii The report in *Army & Navy Gazette*, 6 September 1884, p652 refers, in passing, to Rudolph.

iv Vakeel [Wakil] of Dongola – a deputy, delegate or agent or representative who acts on behalf of a principal.

v Spetchley Park, Worcestershire, home of the Berkeley family.

vi Charles Weld (1812–1885) married 1851 Mary Bland. Charles' brother, Sir Frederick Aloysius Weld married 1859 Philomena Lisle March Phillipps, Ambrose and Laura's daughter.

vii The Weld Memorial Chapel, built by Charles Weld in 1852 in memory of his parents, Humphrey and Christina Weld.

viii Christina and Cecily Weld, eldest daughters of Sir Frederick Weld and Philomena March Phillipps.

ix William Bernard Ullathorne OSB (1806–1889), Bishop of Birmingham 1850–1888.

x Canon Richard Gell Macmullen (1815–1895); ordained as an Anglican minister 1845, member of the Oxford Movement, converted to Catholicism 1 January 1847.

xi Wardour Castle, home of the Arundell family.

xii Cardinal Henry Edward Manning (1808–1892), second Archbishop of Westminster 1865–1892.

xiii Napoléon Eugène Louis Jean Joseph Bonaparte Prince Imperial (1856–1879), only child of Napoleon III, and Empress Eugénie. Trained as a soldier, he served with British forces in the Anglo-Zulu war and was killed in a skirmish. Queen Victoria erected a memorial tomb to his memory in the Chapel, Windsor Castle.

xiv Arthur Bouchard (1845–1896), Chaplain to the voyageurs.

Letter 22: 30 October 1884 –Laura de Lisle to Rudolph

i *Illustrated London News*, 25 October 1884, front cover.

ii Henry Morgan (1830–1912), Master of Jesus College 1885–1912).

iii Rev. William Henry Francklin Hepworth (1832–1918), Vicar of Shepshed 1880–1910.

vi Francis Thomas Eyston (1853–1888) = 17 June 1880 Angela Maria Galdina Vavasour (1854–1930).

v Edward Talbot Wolseley (1848–1935) = 23 January 1872 Florence Mary Weld (1850–1939).

vi Hon. Frances Georgiana Fraser (1826–1899) = 1844 Sir Pyers Mostyn, 8th Baronet (1811–1882).

vii Simon Fraser, 13th Lord Lovat (1828–1887) = Alice Mary Weld-Blundell, daughter of Thomas Weld-Blundell.

viii Laura visited 21–27 September 1861. Talacre Abbey and Talacre Hall, Flintshire, north coast of Wales, built in 1829, home of the Mostyn family until 1919. From 1921–1988 the estate was home to a community of Benedictine nuns, who moved out in 1988, when it once again became a private house and was renamed Westbury Castle.

ix Probably Gertrude Winifred Mostyn (1863–1933).

x Five sons, Pyers William (1846–1912), George Trevor (1857–1913), Thomas Alexander (1859–1938), Nicholas Joseph (1865–1888), and Francis Edward (1860–1939), ordained 14 September 1884.

xi Captain Heygate is possibly Captain Edward Nicholas Heygate (1827–1896).

xii Possibly *General Gordon: Or The Man of Faith* by William Frith, published 1884.

xiii Lieutenant Colonel Sir Henry Trotter, KCMG, CB (1841–1919) of the Royal Engineers. Son of Alexander Trotter (1804–1865) and Jacqueline Elizabeth Otter (1811–1849), sister Amelia Harriet Otter (1817–1890), wife of Edward Strutt, 1st Baron Belper.

Letter 23: 9 March 1885 – Lord (later Admiral) Charles Beresford to Laura de Lisle

i See page 128, for an extract from Lord Charles Beresford's report of the battle in *The London Gazette*, number 25465, dated Tuesday, 28 April 1885.

Rudolph's Sketches in The Illustrated London News

No official agreement existed between Rudolph and the Editors of the *Illustrated London News* for the publication of his sketches. Nor is anything recorded as to how and when the association began, though the first instance appears to have been in the 15 February 1879 issue, wherein they published two sketches of the Pitcairn Islands made by Rudolph in 1873 while on board HMS *Cameleon*.

The relationship was an informal and, occasionally, fractious one. Rudolph seems to have sent his sketches as and when he completed them, with no prior agreement as to the prospect of publication or, indeed, of payment, though he did tell his mother in his 6 January 1885 letter 'still I confess I am sordid enough to wish the editor would communicate with me to my advantage.'

There were difficulties over the fate of the original sketches sent. 'I wrote rather a peremptory letter last time, asking that the sketches might be sent to you, whether used or not: for I know you would value them, knowing the difficulties under which they were done.' [6 January 1885].

Nor was Rudolph always pleased with the results when his sketches were published. Individual sketches were merged into collages, some sketches cut up piecemeal, images reversed, proportions changed, and some elements left out altogether. In his 20 November 1884 letter, he wrote to his mother 'but I must say I was disgusted with the sketches as reproduced of November 1st,' and later on 6 January 1885, after the *Illustrated London News* had sent some of his original sketches back to his mother 'I flatter myself they have not the stiffness of their reproductions.'

Still, he valued the opportunity to have his sketches brought to the wider world, and worried about his future publication prospects as 'Melton Prior, *Illustrated* artist, is also with us, so my sketches would very likely not be in it.' [13 January 1885].

Rudolph continued sketching right up until the end. He wrote to his mother in his final letter of 13 January 1885, 'Some parts of the desert are very pretty, and I think I have in my mind's eye plenty of material for painting' though, as he ruefully noted, 'my sketch book has literally fallen to pieces', and his hands, as he wrote on 20 December 1884 'skinned all over and like raw beef' were still giving him trouble but had recovered sufficiently that, prophetically as it turned out, 'I can hold my sword now if necessary.'

On 31 January 1885, the *Illustrated London News* published Rudolph's obituary with that of his friend, and subject of many of his sketches, Commander Alfred Pigott, who was killed alongside him at Abu Klea.

On 7 February 1885, a final sketch of Rudolph's was printed – a facsimile of an original sketch, reproduced exactly as it was drawn, just as he would have wanted.

Facsimile of a sketch by the late Lt. de Lisle R.N. Appeared in the *Illustrated London News*, 7 February 1885.

Illustrated London News

ORIGINAL SKETCHES AND THEIR PRINTED COUNTERPARTS

Descriptions of the Death of Rudolph de Lisle RN

17 January 1885

1885	Beresford, Lord Charles (1846–1919)	The London Gazette, No. 25465, dated Tuesday, April 28, 1885, pp. 1913–1930. *Report of Proceedings of Naval Brigade from November 26 last to March 8, 1885*	
1914	Beresford, Lord Charles	*The Memoirs of Admiral Lord Charles Beresford*, 2 Volumes, Vol. 1, p. 267	8vo
1975	Gleichen, Count Arthur	*With the Camel Corps Up The Nile*, p. 136	8vo
1989	Barthorp, M.	*Blood Red Desert Sand: Egypt & Sudan 1882–1898*, p. 105 & 107	R.8vo
2005	Asher, M	*Khartoum*, p. 219, 224	8vo

AN EXTRACT FROM THE LONDON GAZETTE
Numb. 25465
Dated Tuesday, April 28, 1885

Korti, March 12, 1885.

Sir,

I HAVE the honour to forward herewith a letter of proceedings of the Naval Brigade, under my command, and to request that should you think fit, you will be pleased to forward the same for the information of the Lords Commissioners of the Admiralty.

I have, &c
CHARLES BERESFORD, Captain.

Major-General
Sir Redvers Buller, V.C.,
Chief of the Staff

Report of Proceedings of Naval Brigade from November 26 last to March 8, 1885.

Korti, March 10, 1885.

Sir

I HAVE the honour to report the proceedings of the Naval Brigade from November 26 last, the day on which I was appointed to take command.

November 26, 1884, to January 5, 1885, the men forming the Naval Brigade were employed on various duties on different parts of the river.

5 January.	The 1st Division under the command of Lieutenant A. Pigott arrived at Korti, I myself arriving from Dal, where I had been employed on duty.
8 January.	The 1st Division left Korti in the column commanded by Brigadier-General Sir Herbert Stewart.
12 January.	Arrived at Gakdul.
14 January.	Left Gakdul with column.
16 January.	In the afternoon we first had touch with the enemy, the Hussar scouts reporting them to be in considerable numbers about 4 miles ahead of the column, which position was 4 or 5 miles distant from Abou-Klea Wells.

The General formed a Zareba for the night. Camels inside, men outside between them and Zareba.

The Naval Brigade were posted with their Gardner on the flank. During that night a continuous and annoying rifle fire was kept up on the Zareba by riflemen from hills on the right flank, distant about 800 yards.

As the morning dawned this fire increased. There were no casualties in the Naval Brigade. 17th January, after breakfast, at 6 a.m., the force was formed up for receiving an attack outside the Zareba, the Artillery (half-battery 7-pr. Screw guns) and Naval Brigade with the Gardner gun taking position on the right front. The fire from the enemy's riflemen increased considerably during this period.

Shortly after 9a.m. the General, having waited for presumed attack, ordered the square to be formed on a clear space, about 400 yards in front of the Zareba. I was directed to place the Gardner gun in the centre of the rear face, keeping it in a line with men marching; but if the square was attacked from the front, or on either of the flanks, I was to use my own judgment as to the best place for the gun. The square advanced under a very hot fire, from the left flank, for about 2 miles, as we cleared a hill on our left flank, flags of different devices, numbering nearly 100 were seen attached to poles planted in the ground amongst the grass, which was high. The edge of the grass, from the flank of the square, was about 400 yards distant, the flags about 700 yards. Not one of the enemy was visible in the grass at this moment. The square halted when abreast the flags, and immediately the enemy, to the number of about 6,000, sprang up from the vicinity of the flags, and formed a V-shaped column with the apex towards the square. They were accompanied by about 40 horsemen, who all carried flags, and came on at a hard gallop; the footmen, who carried spears, swords, or axes, kept pace with them, however.

Immediately I perceived the enemy coming down, I ran the gun from its position in the rear face of the square to a position in the centre of the left flank, about five paces out from the square, and at once commenced firing. After firing about 40 rounds, or eight turns of the lever, I perceived by where the enemy were falling that the gun had too much elevation, so I gave the order 'Cease firing' to alter the elevation. In a moment this was effected, and we had again commenced firing on the front ranks of the enemy with the most excellent results, when, after about 30 rounds, the gun jammed.

The enemy were then about 200 yards from the muzzle of the gun.

The Captain of the gun, Will Rhoods, chief boatswain mate, and myself, unscrewed the plate to clear the barrel, or take the lock of the jammed barrel out, when the enemy were upon us.

Rhoods was killed with a spear. Walter Miller, armourer, I also saw killed with a spear at the same moment on my left. I was knocked down in the rear of the gun, but uninjured, except a small spear scratch on the left hand. The crowd and crush of the enemy was very great at this point, and, as I struggled up, I was carried against the face of the square, which was literally pressed back by sheer weight of numbers about 12 paces from the position of the gun. The crush was so great, that at the moment few on either side were killed, but fortunately this flank of the square had been forced up a very steep little mound, which enabled the rear rank to open a tremendous fire over the heads of the front rank of men; this relieved the pressure and enabled the front rank to bayonet or shoot those of the enemy nearest them. The enemy then, for some reason, turned to their right along the left flank of the square, and streamed away in numbers along the rear face of it, where I afterwards heard they affected an entrance.

None of them got into the square at the place I indicated where the crush was, which was held by the Mounted Infantry. In a very few minutes the terrific fire from the square told on the enemy. There was a momentary waver, and they then walked quietly away. I immediately manned the Gardner, cleared the jam as soon as I could. This, however, was not done in time to be of much use in firing on the slowly retreating enemy, as they had got back into the nullah and behind the mound before it was ready.

After falling in the Brigade, which numbered 40 at the commencement of the action (the remainder having been left behind in the Zareba to guard our gear), I found there were eight killed and seven wounded, among the former being,

I regret to say, two of the most excellent officers in Her Majesty's Service, Lieutenants Alfred Pigott and Rudolf De Lisle, R.N.

After the fight, I found the bodies of these officers, of J. Burleigh and F. Nye, able seamen, together with most of the wounded, about 20 yards to the left rear of the gun outside the square, which led me to believe they were borne away in the crush I have described, when the enemy turned away from the left flank, and headed across the rear face of the square. This was corroborated by some of the wounded.

The report continues to detail subsequent action between January 18 and March 9, concluding:

I attach a complete list of the officers and men forming the Naval Brigade, also a list of those killed and wounded.

I have, &c

(Signed) CHARLES BERESFORD

Captain, R.N.

[NOTE: The gun was jammed by the extractor of the second barrel from the right pulling the head off the empty cylinder of a cartridge which had been fired. The cylinder remaining in the barrel necessarily prevented the new cartridge from being forced home to its place in the barrel.]

RETURN showing the Officers and Men forming the Naval Brigade:—

Korti, March 10, 1885

1st Division.

Captain Lord Charles Beresford.
Lieutenant Alfred Pigott, killed.
Lieutenant Rudolf de Lisle, killed.
Sub-Lieutenant Ed. L. Munro, wounded.
James Webber, boatswain.
1 Chief Petty Officer.
2 1st Class Petty Officers.
1 Signaller.
1 2nd Class Petty Officer.
5 Leading Seamen.
34 A.B.s.
1 Ordinary.
2 Engine Room Artificers.
1 Leading Stoker.
1 Skilled Shipwright.

1 Armourer.
1 Private.
1 Stoker.
Joined on February 11, 1885.
Lieutenant R.A.G. Montgomerie.
Lieutenant G.W. Tyler.

2nd Division.
Lieutenant Ed. Van Koughnet, wounded.
Lieutenant Richard Poore.
Sub-Lieutenant Colin Keppel.
George Sparkes, Engineer.
A. May, Signaller.
Henry Benbow, Chief Engineer.
Sub-Lieutenant Ed. L. Hardy.
6 1st Class Petty Officers.
3 2nd Class Petty Officers.
1 Signaller.
5 Leading Seamen.
26 A.B.s.
1 Ordinary.
2 Engine Room Artificers.
1 Leading Stoker.
1 Stoker.
2 Carpenter's Mates.
1 Private.
Officers. 13.
Men. 101.

CHARLES BERESFORD,
Captain, R.N.

NOMINAL ROLL of Killed and Wounded
Naval Brigade, from 16th January 1885: —
Killed at Abou-Klea, 7th [sic] January 1885

Lieutenant Pigott.
Lieutenant de Lisle.
Chief Boatswain's Mate, F. Rhodes.

Gunner's Mate G. Webb.
Armourer W. Miller.
A.B. E. Soar.
A.B. J. Burney.
A.B. J. Aye.

<u>Killed on S.S. '*Sofia*'</u>
Petty Officer Curnow.

<u>Wounded</u>
19th January 1885.
Lieutenant L. Monro, slightly

3rd February, 1885, S.S. '*Sofia*'
Lieutenant Van Koughnet, severely.

16th February, 1885.
A.B. A. Brewer, severely.

17th January, 1885.
A.B. R. Legg, spear.
A.B. J. Whitehead, spear.
A.B. F. Moore, spear.
A.B. A. Dredge, spear.
A.B. A. H. March, severely
1st Class Petty Officer C. Saysell, spear.
Petty Officer Garland
Petty Officer Woodman, scalded by steam from boiler, penetrated by shot, S.S. 'Sofia'.

(Signed) T.F. O'DWYER, M.D.,
Surgeon-Major, M.S.
P.M.O.N.E.F.

Korti, 15th March, 1885.

FURTHER DESCRIPTIONS OF THE DEATH OF RUDOLPH DE LISLE R.N.
17 January 1885

Asher, M., *Khartoum* p.219 (2005)
'Subsequent action at Abu Klea lasted only 10 minutes', celebrated by Sir Henry Newbolt (1862–1938) in his poem 'Vitai Lampada'

Asher, M. *Khartoum* , p.224 (2005)
'Lieutenant de Lisle had his face hacked clean off by a razor-sharp Dervish sword.'

Barthorp, M. *Blood Red Desert Sand: Egypt & Sudan 1882–1898*, p.105 & 107 (1989)
'The Gardner Jammed. It was instantly overrun, all the sailors being killed.'

Gleichen, Count Arthur, *With the Camel Corps Up The Nile*, p.136 (1975)
'Nine officers killed … Burnaby … Pigott and de Lisle …'

Beresford, Lord Charles, *The Memoirs of Admiral Lord Charles Beresford*, p.267 (1914)
'De Lisle had his whole face cut clean off.'

Funeral Sermon

RUDOLPH de LISLE R.N. (1853–1885)
REQUIEM MASS
MOUNT ST BERNARD ABBEY
FRIDAY, JANUARY 30, 1885

THE SERMON
DELIVERED BY FATHER HENRY COLLINS (1827–1919) OCR
CHAPLAIN OF GRACEDIEU[1]

> How are the valiant fallen in battle! … I grieve for thee, my brother Jonathan, exceeding beautiful and amiable to me, above the love of women. As a mother loveth her only son, so did I love thee. How are the valiant fallen in battle, and the weapons of war perished!
>
> 2 Kings [E.V. 2 Sam.] i. 25–27.

These words form part of the Lamentation which David made over his friend Jonathan, fallen in battle against the Philistines. The words of Scripture are always new. They have a freshness which never fades. They are the echo of the feelings of the human heart in every age and in every clime. They interpret those feelings in a way no other language can in all their wonderful variety. The Bible is a Book we can always turn to for support, consolation, and sympathy. It is the inspired Book of God. The words it contains are not human but divine. It is this that gives them their efficacy, for God alone knows the human heart; He alone can portray the feelings of the human soul. The Scripture is poetry above all other poetry, for it expresses our joy and our sorrows, our regrets and our lamentations, with a force and in a way that no other book can.

In the passage that I have selected there are two things specially portrayed, the beauty of valour and the beauty of love: – 'How are the valiant fallen in battle,' and 'as a mother loveth her only son, so did I love thee'.

Valour and love, as parts of the natural character only, are always beautiful. They are a something to which we cannot refuse our admiration. If a beautiful rosebud withers or sheds its petals on the earth, we mourn for the loss of its beauty; if a grand tree is cut down, and we behold it in its grandeur, prostrate on the ground, we mourn for the loss of its life. But man is not like a plant or a tree; he is created in the image of God. How much more then must we mourn when men are

1. Text taken from: *Memoir of Lieutenant Rudolph de Lisle R.N.* by the Rev. H.N. Oxenham, M.A., London: Chapman and Hall Limited, 1887, pp. 250–263.

cut down in the prime of their life – when a brave man's life is cut short, when those are taken away who possess grand characters and splendid qualities!

We are told of Alexander the Great that one day, on the eve of a battle, he was making a review of his troops, and he was observed to be shedding tears. When asked why he wept, with that splendid display of men before him, he answered that he was thinking how in a few days so many of them would be no more.

It is the natural sentiment to grieve over the brave falling in battle; but it is not merely natural, it is supernatural too. It is not for nothing that the Holy Ghost inspired the writers of the Old Testament to describe the valiant deeds of the brave, and their wonderful courage. God Himself admired them; He admired in men the gifts He Himself had given to them. And so in the Book of Judges we have narrated the various wonders which courage and bravery performed. In the Book of Kings the Holy Ghost gives us a detailed list of David's mighty men, and what they did to win our admiration. And in the Books of Maccabees and other Books of Holy Writ splendid examples of courage are given. God loves an undaunted spirit; He loves in man His own image.

And now we are celebrating the Requiem Mass of one of this noble character – a character very like that of Jonathan, 'exceedingly beautiful', and the words of the text naturally recur to us as again found true, 'How are the valiant fallen in battle! I grieve for thee, my brother Jonathan, exceedingly beautiful and amiable to me, above the love of women. As a mother loveth her only son, so did I love thee. How are the valiant fallen in battle, and the weapons of war perished.'

Rudolph de Lisle chose the profession which he afterwards embraced at an early age. Yet before he finally decided, he had serious doubts if he ought to be a sailor or a priest. It was decided especially by the advice of Bishop Ullathorne that he should be a sailor, and that it would be no unfitting preparation for being a priest later on, if such were God's Will. Now, one might think that these two lives are of an utterly alien character, but they were not so in him. With all his fearlessness and courage Rudolph was thoroughly good to the core, and his life was indeed like the mixture of two lives, that of a sailor and that of a priest. He chose the naval profession, when a boy, because it seemed to offer him a life of daring and adventure, which were the prominent features of his own character. Sailors are generally venturesome and bold. This was his natural character, and these qualities were developed and brought out by the life he had chosen. But he had the bold, frank, and fearless qualities of the sailor, without the coarseness and rudeness which sometimes disfigure the sailor. His whole life was full of brave deeds. This, however, is not the time or place to give a history of many of them, but I shall relate a few. On one occasion when quite young, at the siege of Lima, when the Chilians had nearly destroyed the town, he saw in an upper story a canary in a cage near the window. The house was all on fire, and the canary must necessarily have perished in the flames; Rudolph ventured himself into the burning house, reached the cage, opened it, and released the bird. It flew out and away, but almost immediately returned to its saviour and nestled on his breast for protection. He kept it with him all the day, and then took it to his ship and brought it home with him as a trophy. Even before the Nile Expedition his life was sometimes in imminent danger, whilst carrying out the duties entrusted to him. Once, on the coast of Chili, he was employed in a survey of the locality, whilst war was going on between Chili and Peru, and as he scoured the country on horseback the bullets often whizzed by him, and it was almost a miracle that he escaped.

On the Nile he was always in the front; his boat went first, and this was because his men loved him so, they would do anything for him. The Canadian boatmen some could not manage, but they would do anything at his bidding. In every dangerous undertaking he led the way. Whilst he was on the Nile, one of the boats got loose through the carelessness of the men in charge, and was drifting away, but he at once threw himself into the Nile and went after the boat. He was much bruised and cut by the stones and rocks, but he secured the boat and brought it back, having ventured his life that the men might not be blamed for its loss. His whole life was full of brave deeds. Ever full of energy, he stopped for nothing. His life and character were such as to compel admiration. Strangers who were in his company only a few days or a few hours were struck with admiration. We may be sure, although particulars of how he fell have not yet reached us, we may be sure that it was in the front, that he fronted and led his men in battle with the same bravery that he had already evinced in the labours of the Expedition of the Nile.

But in speaking of his character his valour must not put his lovingness and loveableness out of sight. These, as in Jonathan, were striking features of the beautifulness of his disposition. His sweet, gentle, loving temper, and his daring bravery added lustre to each other, setting each other off like two contrasting colours side by side. Father Lacordaire says: 'You want to be loved – love then, and you will be loved in return.' This was Rudolph's secret of making himself so loveable – he loved. His love was shown most where love should be most shown – at home. He loved his mother more than all else. When he was at home it was her room that he chose to be in, and he made himself a sort of nest in one of its corners, with his drawing implements around him. Her private room was his home. But it was not his mother only whom he loved. He waited tenderly on his father during his last illness. He was the great favourite of his eldest brother, and he loved all his brothers and sisters, and was much loved by them; and he used to go great distances when able so as to give them and himself the pleasure of meeting together for a few days. Friends too, he loved intensely, putting himself to great trouble and expense on their account. But his affection did not stop here. His heart was wide and large, and out of the plentifulness of his love he poured love around him everywhere without stint. He loved his ship companions, the tars and blue-jackets, and they were so fond of him in return that they would do anything for him; but he never took advantage or asked anything of them, which he himself was unwilling to do. On one occasion, when a midshipman only, he was on the watch during the night, in the height of a storm, and one of the masts laden with sail was carried away. Before the end of the watch the captain came up and seeing what had happened was very angry, and asked the midshipman what he meant by having allowed such a thing to happen, and why he had not sent someone up to reef the sail. Rudolph replied: 'I would not have dared to do it myself, and what I would not dare myself I would never ask another to do. It would have been at the imminent risk of a man's life to attempt it, and a man's life is worth more than a mast.' The captain went away still fuming with anger, but in a short time returned and said to Rudolph, 'You were right and I was wrong; a man's life is of more value than a mast, and I wish every one did like you – it would be far better.'

No wonder his men loved him, when he was so thoughtful for them. They knew he took his full share in anything arduous or dangerous. Plutarch in his Lives of Celebrated Men makes this remark: that, if a general wants his soldiers to serve under him with great fidelity and ardour, he must make them love him, and that the way to make them love him is not by handsome presents, by food or clothing, but he must put himself at the head of them in every perilous or laborious undertaking, and they will then vie with one another in doing all to serve him. This was the way Rudolph gained the love of those under him. It was his grand soul that was loveable, and his large far–reaching love spreading itself in plenty to all around, to every one.

Father Faber says that God builds his graces upon the foundation of nature. He does not change the natural character or overturn it, but His supernatural graces have an analogy with the natural character. So it was with Rudolph. Sometimes he loved those much with whom one might have thought he would have had nothing in common. When at the Naval Academy at Gosport, being then only twelve years old, he used to spend his Sundays with an old Italian priest, Dr. Baldaconi, and they grew very fond of each other. He was early at the church and constituted himself the sacristan, serving the Mass, arranging the candles for Benediction, and during the day talking to the old priest, who called him 'the little angel of his congregation'. Later on when he was a young man at Greenwich, he made the acquaintance of some Sisters of Charity in the neighbourhood, and used to pass his Sundays a good deal with them, learning many a lesson of virtue from them. Such friendships seem to the worldly eye rather incongruous, but these Sisters of Charity knew what they were doing; St. Vincent of Paul their founder used to say of them that their veil was their cloister. Their veil marks them out in the camp or on the battlefield as consecrated to God. Thus living above the world in its very midst they could afford to let this young naval officer come to see them, encouraging in him that noble and pious disposition which his frank simplicity made so very graceful in him.

When at Malta, later on, he interested himself in a Convent of the Little Sisters of the Poor, and when a bazaar was organized there to help them in their charities, not being able to give them money, he made some water-colour paintings for them, one of his own ship which fetched several pounds, and this was his contribution to their work. So it was that he mingled his love with the works of monks and nuns, sharing their desire for the things of God, and being drawn to them because of their pure, kind, and holy examples. He was as fond of being with those devoted to the service of God as with those of his own profession. He had a great hatred of sin, and when one of his friends had committed before the world a great public scandal, Rudolph said he would gladly have given his life to save him from this offence.

His brave spirit often showed itself in the manner in which he stood up for his religion; seeing on one occasion the men of his ship going on shore to attend the Protestant service, it struck him that some Catholics might be amongst them, who, for the pleasure of going ashore, were willing to go to the Protestant church. So he said aloud; 'I expect, captain, that some of the men are Catholics, and by the regulations ought to be allowed to go to Mass.' The captain was not pleased, but not being able to contradict the truth of the assertion, he called out that if any of the men were Catholics, they should stand out apart. Twelve men accordingly fell out, and were sent on shore to the Catholic church under the charge of Rudolph, who was then only a midshipman, just having entered the service. After this, when there was no Mass to go to, the Catholics came into the captain's cabin where he read the Mass prayers for them and a sermon too. If he had no sermon in a book, he made an exhortation himself, and he used to say laughing that he thought he could preach pretty well, and might still perhaps eventually become a priest. We know that in England the Catholic religion is in a minority, and it requires a great deal of courage at times to stand up faithfully for one's religion; many would never dare to do so. Rudolph not only dared it, but thought nothing of it. He was so simple that it seemed never to occur to him that he had done anything wonderful. Yet the things that seemed nothing to him filled those who saw or heard them with stupefied amazement.

On another occasion, later on, there was a French man-of-war stationed not far from his ship in one of the harbours of the Pacific Ocean, and as there was Mass on board this ship Rudolph thought it best to take the men to hear Mass there, rather than go on shore. Leave was asked and obtained; so a quarter of an hour before the time he arrived with his men. He himself was invited by the officers at once into the cabin, where they showed him every politeness. But by and bye, the quarter of an hour being expired, Rudolph looking at his watch said, 'Ah, I see it's Mass time now.' These

French officers were Catholics, but lived as too many of the French do in total disregard of religion. They never expected the young English officer would himself go to Mass, but that he would only see that his men did. So when Rudolph said: 'It is Mass time,' they replied, 'Mass! surely you are not going to Mass?' 'Yes I am,' said Rudolph, and at once taking leave he went off and entered the place where Mass was to be said. About the time of the Sanctus, one of the French officers slunk in. The next Sunday two or three came in; the Sunday after the whole of the officers attended Mass from the very commencement, and they continued to do so for the six weeks longer that the two men–of–war were within easy reach of each other.

Rudolph thus rode over every obstacle that came in the way of his professing his religion. He did not mind whether he was despised or not for his faith. Now Jesus Christ has said, 'He that confesseth me before men, him will I confess before My Father and the holy angels.' When a soldier dies in battle, he is not able, perhaps, to make his confession, or to have the help of a priest for the sacraments, and Rudolph died as a soldier though in the naval service. But two months before he did go to Holy Communion. The Canadians on the Expedition had a priest with them, and on his birthday, November 23rd, an altar was made under a tree in the desert, and the Holy Mass was said, and Rudolph went to Communion.

We all sin daily, and like the rest of men no doubt Rudolph committed some other sins before he died, but we may be sure Almighty God never let him die in mortal guilt. He had confessed Christ boldly and intrepidly before men; he had been bold for his Lord and Saviour, and God would never leave him unprotected in the hour of trial. But no doubt he was at times drawn away more or less into the vortex around him, and we ought to pray for him that he may soon pass through his Purgatory and be admitted into the presence of his Lord.

But happy are they that confess their Lord so well in this life, and leave such fair and noble examples; and happy is the mother of such noble children. It is said of Cornelia, the mother of the Gracchi, that when another Roman lady after showing off her trinkets said to her, 'Where now are your jewels?' her two boys came in from school at that moment, and Cornelia replied 'These are my jewels, educated in virtue for the good of their country.' A mother that has good, noble children shall never be ashamed when she speaks with her enemies in the gate. Let us pray, however, and offer Masses for the soul of young Rudolph, and gain indulgences, that every spot being clean burnished away, he may become a vessel meet for the Master's table.

Will of Rudolph de Lisle Lieut. RN

NAVAL CAMP, ABKA 24TH OCTOBER 1884[1]

'By last mail I sent my will, which I trust is not necessary just yet, but might be; anyway, as well to have it made out.'
Letter: 1 November 1884

(A)
I wish the £1400 lent to the late A. C. de Lisle of Garendon Park & Grace Dieu Manor when paid back by his successor Everard de Lisle (the present possessor) to be divided equally between Edwin Margaret and Gerard de Lisle

(B)
1000£ insurance paid on death of Frank de Lisle of W. Australia after deducting lawyers fees & expenses connected with transferring the money from West Australia to Mess.[rs] Berich Davidson & Co to be paid as follows –

100£ or as much more as may be required to settle my debts

To my goddaughter Mary Cannon daughter of D.[r] Cannon (late R.N.) (Physician Valparaiso) Chili 25£ (twenty–five pounds)

To M[rs] Frank de Lisle (widow) 100£. M[rs] Francis Kerr widow of the late (Major Francis Kerr & my intimate friend) of Conadino Malta 50£

Remainder or residue between Edwin Margaret & Gerard de Lisle equally – Rudolph de Lisle Lieut. R.N. – Witnesses Francis Hungerford Pollen Sub-Lieut. R.N. – Arthur W. May Surgeon R.N.

Affidavit of due execution filed

On the 4th day of November 1885 Admon with this Will annexed of the effects of the deceased was granted to Edwin Joseph Lisle March Phillipps (in the Will written Edwin) de Lisle Esquire and Gerard Lisle March Phillipps (in the Will written Gerard) de Lisle Esquire the natural and lawful brothers of the said deceased.

Ad. Will
BE IT KNOWN that Rudolph otherwise Rudolph Edward de Lisle March Phillipps de Lisle late of One Barrow Lodge near Leicester in the county of Leicester Esquire a Lieutenant in the Royal Navy deceased, who died on the 17th day of January 1885 near the Abu Klea Wells in the Soudan Africa a Bachelor with Father, made and duly executed

1. Enclosed with his letter to his mother, Laura, dated 25 October 1884.

his last Will and Testament and did not therein name an Executor or Residuary Legatee. That Eleanor Maria March Phillips de Lisle the natural and lawful Mother and only next of kin of the said Deceased has renounced the Letters of Administration with the said Will of the personal estate of the said Deceased.

AND BE IT FURTHER KNOWN, that at the date hereunder written, Letters of Administration with the Will of the personal estate of the said Deceased were granted by Her Majesty's High Court of Justice at the Principal Registry of the Probate Division thereof to Edwin Joseph March Phillipps (in the Will written Edwin) de Lisle of One Barrow Lodge aforesaid Esquire and Gerard Lisle March Phillipps (in the Will written Gerard) de Lisle of One Barrow Lodge aforesaid Esquire the natural and lawful Brothers of the said Deceased they having first been sworn well and faithfully to administer the same.

Dated the 4th day of November 1885.

Gross value of personal estate, £2503–15–7.

Mentioned in the Will

- Ambrose Charles de Lisle (1834–1883); Rudolph's eldest brother; oldest son of Ambrose and Laura de Lisle.
- Everard de Lisle (1862–1947); Rudolph's nephew, son of Ambrose Charles de Lisle and his first wife Frances Amelia Victoria Sutton (1840–1871).
- Edwin de Lisle (1852–1920); Rudolph's older brother, 13th of the 16 children of Ambrose and Laura de Lisle.
- Margaret de Lisle (1855–1895); Rudolph's youngest sister who later in life became a nun; 15th of the 16 children of Ambrose and Laura de Lisle.
- Gerard de Lisle (1860–1924); Rudolph's youngest brother, 16th and last of the children of Ambrose and Laura de Lisle.
- Francis (Frank) de Lisle (1851–1883); Rudolph's older brother, 12th of the 16 children of Ambrose and Laura de Lisle.
- Mrs Francis de Lisle, née Emma Thomson (1861–1899), remarried 1886.
- Dr Richard Cannon R.N. (retired) (1841–1927).
- Mary Cannon
- Major Francis Kerr (1840–1884); of the Rifle Brigade.
- Mrs Francis Kerr, née Mary Frances Monteith (d. 1916); married Major Kerr 4 October 1870.
- Francis Hungerford Pollen R.N. (1862–1944); Sub-Lieutenant on HMS *Alexandra* and part of the Naval Brigade on The Nile Expedition.
- Arthur W. May R.N. (1854–1925); Surgeon on HMS *Alexandra* and part of the Naval Brigade on The Nile Expedition. Later Sir Arthur William May KCB, FRCS, Surgeon Vice-Admiral, Late Medical Director General, Medical Department of the Navy, Honorary Physician to the King.

The Mortuary Card of Rudolph de Lisle Lieut. RN

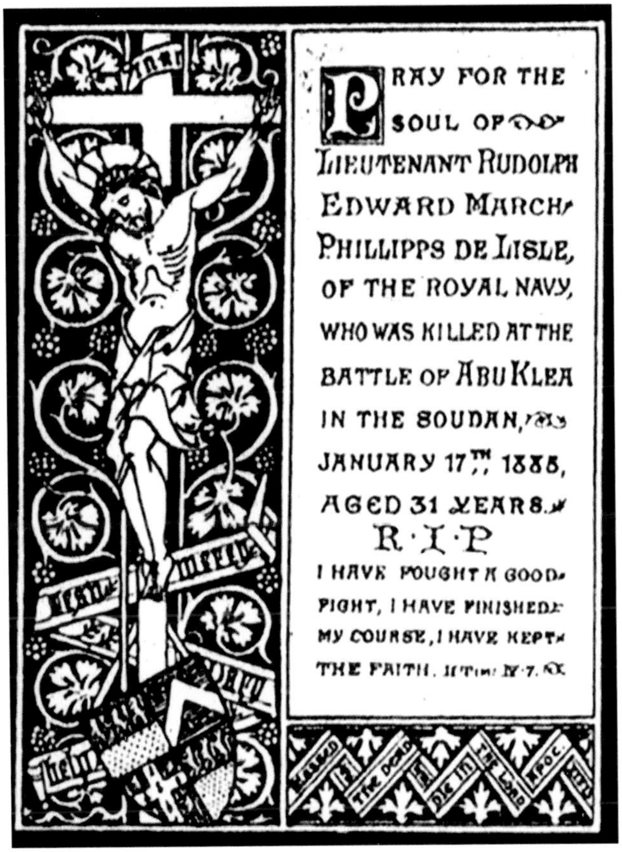

Mortuary card in commemoration of Rudolph, handed to attendees of his memorial service and sent to those family and friends unable to attend.

Epilogue

I trust the data, letters and pictures will have interested you – as it has me over many years collecting them – and many thanks to the family (numerous gifts over time), Miss Boniface for her laborious endeavour, and finally to Pen & Sword for their patience and diligence.

I am blessed to be able to have all this published and therefore saved for posterity since much of the originals are very faint or frail.

Rudolph I had a namesake: Rudolph II (1892–1943) who became a Lieutenant Commander after the First World War and died in 1943, never having fully recovered from being sunk in 1916.

I trust they would both be pleased by this book and I wish you all a pleasant read; this will become – I hope – the last volume of a trilogy. The first tome will be an Illustrated Account of Rudolph I's several trips round our little world! To be published, I hope, in 2025!

Gerard de Lisle
Cold Newton Lodge
January 2024

Appendices

Appendix I

ABU KLEA REVISITED

by Drummer Alexander Bourne-May
The Honourable Artillery Company

Reprinted with the kind permission of *The Guards Magazine*: *Journal of the Household Division*, Summer 2016.

Having been fascinated with the battles fought by the British in Sudan since I first saw the 1939 version of *The Four Feathers*, I was determined to take advantage of currently living relatively close by in Dubai by making a trip to the Sudan to visit the battlefields. Luckily for myself, the timing was extremely fortuitous and, following a very kind invitation from the current Defence Attaché in Khartoum, Lieutenant Colonel Edward Melotte, Irish Guards, I was able to join him and a small group of embassy staff and family members on a planned excursion to the battlefield at Abu Klea.

The site itself is remote, being an 8-hour drive north of Khartoum, mostly off-road and through open desert where, if you do chance across a small site of habitation, it is most likely you'll see Sudanese villagers living and surviving in a way little changed to that of their ancestors at the time of the battle 131 years ago. When approaching Abu Klea and the battlefield, the surrounding countryside changes dramatically from flat desert to undulating ground of black stone which presents an almost lunar landscape.

The battle itself took place on 17 January 1885 during the ill-fated campaign to relieve Major General Charles Gordon in Khartoum, and was to be the bloodiest engagement British forces fought on Sudanese soil. Whilst the main relief force, under the command of Sir Garnet Wolseley, was to travel up the Nile to Khartoum, a desert column commanded by Major General Sir Herbert Stewart was dispatched across the Bayuda desert as an advance force to Metemmah, from which a small number of troops would board steamers and proceed directly to Khartoum by river to provide support whilst the main force followed up.

The desert column consisted of the Camel Corps formed from four regiments: the Heavy Camel Regiment (including elements of 1st and 2nd Life Guards and the Royal Horse Guards), the Guards Camel Regiment (a composite body of Foot Guards and Royal Marine Light Infantry) plus the Light and Mounted Infantry Camel Regiments. In addition, the column included the 1st Battalion the Sussex Regiment and a detachment from 19th Hussars as well as three guns from the Royal Artillery and a Gardner Gun (an early machine gun), manned by men of the Royal Navy.

The plan to cut across the desert from one stretch of the Nile to another meant that the column was totally reliant on the capture of certain wells in order to re-supply with water. One of these wells was situated within the Abu Klea wadi (a valley known as Abu Tulayh by the locals). Stewart was not expecting resistance at the wells, presuming that the Mahdist forces would make their stand at Metemmah. It was therefore an unexpected shock when a large force of Dervishes was reported as sitting between the column and the wells on 16 January. The estimated strength of the Dervishes was 13,000 whilst the desert column consisted of approximately 1,400 men. Stewart prepared his force for an imminent attack on the afternoon of 16 January. The troops built a hasty fortification, known as a *zariba*, consisting of a square of stone two feet high which still exists to this day.

The attack by the Mahdist forces never took place but the British were continually harassed by Dervish sniper fire throughout the night and early morning. Once it became clear that the enemy attack would not materialise, at 10am on 17 January, Stewart ordered the column to advance in square formation in order to take the wells by force. The depleted state of the column's water supply meant that there was no choice but to advance on the wells and succeed in their capture.

The wells themselves sit in the far end of the wadi, and the Dervishes anticipated that the British force would advance straight down the wadi, leading them into a perfect position to be ambushed by the Dervishes' vastly superior numbers (this had been the case with previous victories over British-led Egyptian armies). However, Stewart chose instead to advance along the high ground running parallel to the wadi.

The battlefield today is unchanged (with the exception of a diminished number of trees in the wadi) and it is easy to follow the advance of the British square from their encampment, along the high ground towards the wells. The ground is rocky and uneven with a number of shallow ravines that create dead ground in which hundreds or indeed thousands of attackers could be concealed. Across this terrain the column advanced in square, knowing that its strength lay in keeping its formation solid, a task made all the more difficult by the slow pace of the camels, including those carrying the wounded from the previous day.

The column was harassed by Dervish sniping throughout its advance, with skirmishers from the Mounted Infantry sent out to deal with this threat as best they could. Although accounts and theories differ as to why, the rear left of the square lost its rigid formation, with elements of the Heavy Camel Regiment and the Naval Gardner Gun effectively outside the protection of the now open square (as described in Samantha Wyndham's excellent article on the subject in the Winter 2015/16 edition of *The Guards Magazine*).

At this point, after an advance of a mile and a half, the front of the square crested a knoll that concealed between three and four thousand Dervishes. These warriors were of the Baggara tribe, renowned fighters who were viewed as the best of the Mahdi's army. These warriors rose up and charged the front left corner of the square. In order to gain clearer fields of fire, the square hastily moved half right and halted on the top of a slight incline. The position was perfect except for a ravine which allowed the enemy a covered approach to within 180 metres of the square. However, it also gave the advantage of breaking their ranks as they charged. On the ground the battlefield seems to be an almost featureless open landscape, however, with the use of a few maps and books for reference, it is easily possible to work out the rough positions of the square to within 50 yards. The close proximity of the Dervish charge is striking. Once in position the square was within 100 yards of the Dervishes. Today the Abu Klea memorial marks the approximate spot where the front left of the square stood.

As the Dervishes advanced, the Mounted Infantry (on the front left of the square) opened fire, and as Bill Burge of the Guards Camel Regiment later described: 'The sides of the square literally blazed with fire.' This fire was devastating, with no hope of reaching the square, the Dervishes soon began to falter. However, the rear left of the square was still in disarray and as some described it, the Baggara warriors wheeled, almost in a parade ground manoeuvre, under fire, and struck at the rear left of the square. This part of the square was occupied by the Heavy Camel regiment, because these were the men with the least experience when it came to fighting in square and had therefore been placed in the least exposed rear section. When the Dervishes struck, the 3rd Company of the Regiment (made up of men of 5th Dragoon Guards, along with the famed Colonel Fred Burnaby, Royal Horse Guards and the naval Gardner Gun), were isolated and engulfed by the mass of Dervish warriors; many did not make it back to the square.

Soon a desperate fight developed with Baggara tribesmen breaking into the gap in the square and wreaking havoc within. The men of the Mounted Infantry as well as the rest of the Heavy Camel Regiment (including the Life Guards and Royal Horse Guards) had to turn and fire into the square as well as fend off tribesmen in bitter hand–to–hand combat.

Meanwhile the Guards Camel Regiment on the front right corner of the square was largely unaware, beyond the noise of fighting, as to what was happening. Once on the battlefield, one can appreciate that the size of the square and the rise and fall in the ground and the mass of camels in the centre would have obscured much of the view. Lieutenant Count Albert Gleichen of the Grenadier Guards (later to become a major general in the First World War) describes the point at which the guardsmen felt the impact of the Dervish attack into the rear of the square: 'The camels inside the square obstructed all vision to the fighting flank, and we had already concluded that the fire of the Heavies and Mounted Infantry had swept back the Arabs, when suddenly a terrific shock was felt, accompanied by redoubled yells and firing. I found myself lifted off my legs amongst a surging mass of Heavies and Sussex who had been carried back against the camels by the impetuous rush of the enemy.'

After 15 minutes of pitched battle the British had reformed the square, and succeeded in repulsing the Dervish attack with Gleichen describing the fighting as 'swarms of Arabs in desperate hand-to-hand fight with our men, hacking, hewing, hamstringing and yelling like black devils on a ground literally piled with the dead and dying'. The British were only saved from disaster by the discipline of the soldiers on the front and right ranks of the square, including the Guards Camel Regiment, who held fast and were able to fire successive volleys on the Dervishes who had broken into the British formation.

No Dervishes that entered the square were left alive. The vast majority of the 74 British fatalities of the day were incurred at the rear left of the square and came from the Heavy Camel Regiment and the naval crew of the Gardner Gun. Amongst them was Colonel Burnaby who was mortally wounded and died within minutes of the repulse of the Dervishes. Approximately 1,100 Dervishes lay dead on the battlefield.

With the repulse of the Dervishes the square prepared for another attack, but it never came. Instead the incessant sniping which had occurred for much of the morning continued. Whilst the Guards Camel Regiment had not taken any serious casualties during the Dervish attack, after the battle Gleichen described the point that one of his men was hit by a Dervish bullet: 'One of our best men (Ormiston, 3rd Grenadiers) was shot by one of these brutes. As he was handing his water bottle to another man a bullet passed through his friend's hand and pierced his chest. He fell on to me, a torrent of blood gushing out of his mouth. No use trying to staunch it; he was dead in less than a minute.'

With time the Dervish fire melted away and the British began to collect weapons, tend to the wounded and bury their dead. There are a large number of graves at the battlefield to this day. It is unclear whose graves they are, but it is thought most likely that they are mainly Muslim, with several accounts claiming the British buried their dead in a mass grave outside the square. It is said that the largest cairn visible at the battlefield is that of Burnaby's, because every soldier of the column placed a stone on it as they moved off the battlefield.

The graves and the memorial to the British dead which stands on the site are not the only evidence of the fighting that took place here. Our party was also able to unearth half a dozen spent Martini Henry cartridge cases in as many minutes. This is a site that is rarely visited and one that remains all but untouched since the events of 17 January 1885.

Once ready to move, the column descended into the wadi, reaching their objective, the wells, at 5pm. These are now a collection of approximately 40 small sink holes, and not so easily identified. They are still used by the locals, and we were fortunate to come across two camel herders watering their livestock at one of them.

The men of the desert column went on to endure a freezing and restless night at the wells followed by a difficult forced march to Metemmah through the night of 18 January. The force faced another day of harassing fire whilst camped overlooking the outskirts of Metemmah which resulted in the mortal wounding of Major General Stewart. This was followed by another battle fought in square on 19 January, the Battle of Abu Kru, which, although by no means an easy fight, went off without the complications and casualties of Abu Klea. As a result, the force occupied Metemmah and a relief force from the Royal Sussex Regiment was dispatched to Khartoum. However, it was ultimately too late, arriving in Khartoum on 28 January. Khartoum had fallen two days before and Gordon had been killed, bringing to an end the 1885 campaign. It was not until 1898 at the Battle of Omdurman that the British (amongst them 1st Battalion Grenadier Guards) would finally defeat the Mahdi's successor, the Khalifa, and take Khartoum thus restoring British honour.

In Khartoum and Omdurman today a number of sites still exist from the days of Gordon and the Battle of Omdurman, providing evidence of the Mahidist campaigns fought by the British. There is also a Commonwealth War Graves Commission site in Khartoum, created in 1960 and bringing together a multitude of graves that had been scattered across pre-independence Sudan. In the cemetery a memorial can be found to the officers and men of the Guards Brigade which fought in the Suakin campaign of 1885. In addition, there are the individual graves of Guardsmen killed, both in the 1885 campaign as well as those of Coldstreamers stationed in the country in 1909 and 1932. The lovingly maintained cemetery provides a permanent reminder of the British military involvement in the country and the part that officers and soldiers of the Guards regiments played during those campaigns.

Appendix II

A BITTER WAIL FROM THE SOUDAN

On 10 February 1885, Sir Henry Newbolt (1862–1938), who in 1892 was to write *Vitai Lampada*, sent Laura de Lisle 'with the profound respect and sympathy of the Author' a copy of his poem 'A Bitter Wail from the Soudan', which he had written just a few weeks before.

Laura's response to the work is not known, however the poem was soon to garner much wider attention.

On 26 February 1885, a letter to the Editor appeared in the Correspondence section of *The Derby Telegraph*. Under the heading 'Tory Abuse of Mr. Gladstone. The Poet of the Jingoes Again at Work', an anonymous contributor, who signed himself as 'Observer' wrote of the 'animus displayed against Mr. Gladstone and the Liberal Government, who have been, and are, hated with a hatred implacable and deadly.'

In illustration of this 'bitter, unrelenting hate entertained towards Mr. Gladstone even by our local Tories, I beg, sir, to enclose for your personal, and also for publication in your popular journal, a copy of a number of handbills, which have been printed in Derby, and quietly distributed by local Tory agents at various public-houses and other places in the town, and which for course, indecent, vituperation and profanity has seldom been equalled in party warfare.'

There followed the text of the offending poem in full, the supposedly outraged 'Observer' thereby managing to bring the poem to the attention of a far wider audience than the denizens of a few pubs. 'A Bitter Wail from the Soudan' went on to be printed in newspapers up and down the country.

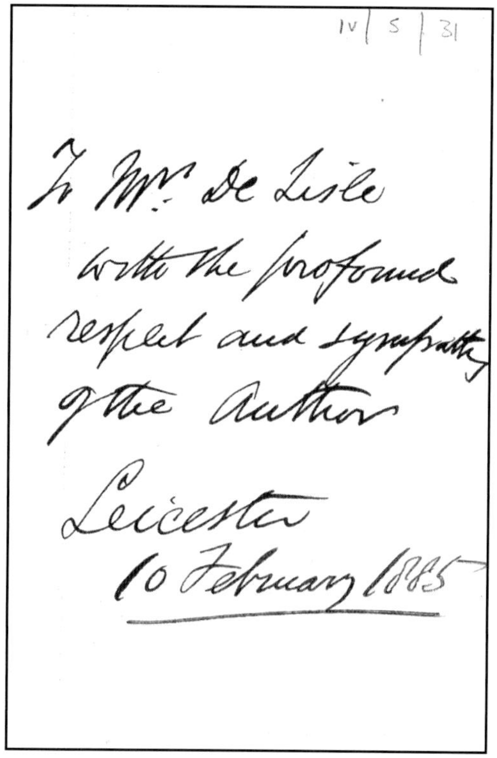
1V / 5 / 31

To Mrs De Lisle
with the profound
respect and sympathy
of the Author

Leicester
10 February 1885

Sir Henry Newbolt's handwritten note to Rudolph's mother, Laura, accompanying a copy of his poem 'A Bitter Wail to the Soudan'.

A BITTER WAIL FROM THE SOUDAN.

27th January, 1885.

Now let the curse of England fall on cruel Gladstone's head ;
The widow's tears, the orphan's wail, the blood of all the dead.
Midlothian's heart, now sore with grief, bemoans herself – betrayed,
Beguiled, misled, deceived by all the promises he made.
Ye brave ones fallen, and your foes, in one vast crowd arise
And haunt his nightly dreams, and scare sweet slumber from his eyes!
What care has he for those he sent to such a needless war?
He who ne'er braved the slightest wound, nor bore the slightest scar;
He who at home in luxury enjoyed his princely ease,
Vaunted his prayers, his charity, and skill in felling trees;
A Pharisee with folded hands and eyes uplift afar;
Who strains at glint of dynamite and swallows Ghouls of war;
Who hoards his pay while thousands starve, yet by the people's will (?)
He gives them in the place of food an empty Franchise Bill!
How came it such a *thing* as he should wield such power so long?
Drunk with his own verbosity, and length and strength of tongue.
Ye noble soldiers, honoured dead, have you no friends to raise
The cry for *his* damnation, the requiem in *your* praise ?
Shall Stewart, De Lisle, and Burnaby, with all the braves they led,
Bleach on the desert sands in vain – sacred though shroudless dead?
Are England's sons completely deaf to lamentations wild
From mothers, sisters, mourning homes, the widow and her child?
Shall he who pressed the traitor's hand to win the traitor's aid
Still govern Englands trembling fate – indifferent, undismayed ?
Shall he who stole the diadem, and sneaked by lies to power,
Be honoured still in England? No! Now make the craven cower –
Let Cavendish and Burke arise from their untimely fate,
Avenged by Justice, slow yet sure – though sure, alas! too late!
Ring in his ear 'Majuba Hill' and 'Alexandria's Flame',
His Oathless constitution, tried in Freedom's holy name.
El Teb and Tokar, Sinkat too, and now to share their doom,
The lion-hearted Gordon, with the people of Khartoum,
Rise up, gaunt fearless spectres, and form your dauntless line!
Ye need no arms for such a foe, no traitors to combine;

All true-born Britons who still live and love their nation's laws
Will join you in the battle for their Queen and Honour's cause.
I fear I see brave Gordon, too, coming to lead you on,
Bedecked with trophies all 'too late', so bravely, nobly won.
How grieved, and sad, and stern his face – I think I hear him say
Can this indelible disgrace be ever washed away ?'
Advance! and Charge! and as you charge shout forth a demon yell
'Down with the heartless Gladstone, and hound him home to Hell!'
Onward they rush, no smoke, no clang of arms, the Despot's gone –
Old England's honour deeply stained, but scatheless stands her throne.
Bravo ! brave souls, you've done your work, now soar on glory high,
'Twas Beaconsfield who waved you on for—
EMPIRE AND LIBERTY.

Appendix III

LIEUTENANT RUDOLPH DE LISLE, R.N.[1]

Taken from *The Month: A Catholic Magazine and Review*, Vol. LVIII, September–December 1886, pp. 495–504.

RUDOLPH EDWARD LISLE MARCH PHILLIPPS DE LISLE was born at Gracedieu Manor, on November 23, 1853, and was the youngest but two of a large family. The first distinct glimpse we have of him in the pages of his biography, shows us a 'lovely fair–haired child of four years old, clad in a red cassock and surplice, serving as acolyte in the beautiful chapel at Gracedieu.' A little later on we have a second, and scarcely less significant picture of a bright fearless boy, whose delight it was to accompany his elder brothers in their sailing expeditions during a stay which the family made at Whitby. His favourite amusement from this time forward was to make and float toy boats, and his love of the sea, thus early acquired, never left him, but, on the contrary, grew and strengthened until it expanded into a vocation so distinct, as to leave his parents no doubt as to the manner of life for which God had destined their son, in whose youthful breast the two passions, devotion to the service of God and love of a seafaring career – which were to rule him throughout his whole future course – had thus plainly manifested themselves, and thus early developed into life.

One other point in reference to the childish years of the future lieutenant must not be passed over, not only because in this instance, also, the child was father to the man, but because it so forcibly illustrates the truth of the French proverb, *bon sang ne ment pas*. Never, his nurse informs us, was he known to tell an untruth, and what is more, never did he practise any of those deceptions, sometimes harmless enough, which many children, who are incapable of uttering a downright lie, allow themselves to commit, from fear of punishment, or a desire to ward off the evil consequences of some thoughtless action. Rudolph, on the contrary, far from attempting to conceal what he had done wrong, anticipated detection by a frank avowal, and his chief, if not his only fault, then as in his later years, was a hastiness of temper, which however tended rather to endear him to those about him, on account of the open-hearted generosity he showed in making reparation to any one whom he feared to have hurt or annoyed.

In September, 1865, he joined his elder brothers at Oscott, where he stayed a twelvemonth, there making his First Communion and receiving Confirmation. On this latter occasion he chose for himself the names of Aloysius Sebastian, and surely these two glorious patrons showed themselves unremitting in their watchful care of one who was always remarkable alike for purity of heart and life and for undaunted courage, both moral and physical. We shall soon see him give abundant proof of his possession of both these virtues. In October, 1866, he was taken to the Royal Naval and Military Academy at Gosport to be prepared for admission into the *Britannia*, and though he gave great satisfaction to his teachers and speedily became a favourite with his companions, he nevertheless found himself placed in a very trying

1. *Life of Lieutenant Rudolph de Lisle, R.N.* By the Rev. H. N. Oxenham, M.A.

position. With the exception of his year at Oscott, he had never before left home, and now he was the only Catholic among ninety boys. Yet not only did he never flinch from the consistent practice of his religious duty; but, what was perhaps even more difficult, especially for a young boy, he contrived to put down the evil habit prevalent among the pupils who slept in the same room with him, of indulging in objectionable conversation after they were in bed. Many a good, well-meaning boy would have so hopelessly mismanaged the affair, that the only result of his attempt would have been to draw down endless ridicule upon himself, but Rudolph's tact and ingenuity were equal to his courage and determination. He proposed to his companions that they should tell each other stories in turn, and offered to lead the way with a narrative out of his favourite *Arabian Nights*. Eagerly was he listened to, night after night, until he suggested that the others should take their turn, the end of the matter being that the evil talk ceased altogether, at least while he was there. *O si sic omnes!*

On the 9th of the following April 'he passed in the first class, sixth out of sixty-five candidates for admission to the *Britannia* training-ship, which he joined at Dartmouth on the 2nd of May,' remaining there till after his final examination at the end of July, 1868, when he joined the *Victory* at Portsmouth. In reference to his sojourn on board the *Britannia*, we cannot refrain from giving the following extract from a letter to his mother written during that period, and showing in regard to his religious duties at once careful conscientiousness and also that practical common sense which is ever found to accompany all true sanctity. 'I cannot,' he says, 'manage ever to go Communion more than once a month, which I always do. One Sunday I could not even go to Mass on account of the rain. I do my best always to go to Mass and the sacraments as often as I am able, so I cannot do more than I am able.' What God enabled his loyal and true-hearted servant to do, both for his own soul, and also for the souls of those under his command, will be seen in the course of this brief sketch, but we may fitly place here an incident, too striking and also too edifying to be omitted. It occurred while he was on board the *Bristol*, to which he had been transferred from the *Victory*, September 2, 1868, and he was, at the time it happened, not yet sixteen years of age. We will give it in the words of one who was an officer with him at the time in the Channel Fleet, though in another ship:

> In 1869 he and I were attached to the Channel Fleet, lying at Lisbon. Each Sunday I met de Lisle at Mass with his men. Upon one Sunday the sermon was on confession, preached by a Father Duckett, who wound up his discourse with a strong and eloquent appeal to each of us not to delay a moment in going to confession if in a state of mortal sin. Young de Lisle immediately left his seat in face of a congregation of some two hundred blue-jackets and half a dozen officers and entered the confessional. His example shamed three other officers and myself into following his example, though we had not the pluck to do it in the open way he did. We were twenty-two to thirty years of age (pp. 144, 145).

Truly one is at a loss what to admire most, as one peruses the above record, the total absence of human respect, the unfeigned humility which made the youthful sailor not pause to remember that, by entering the confessional after such words had been uttered he might expose himself to the imputation of being in a state of mortal sin, or the delicate charity which caused him to think solely of how he might set a good example, and make it easy for any of his companions who might unhappily be in a state of enmity to God, to reconcile themselves with Him.

From this time until April, 1875, when Rudolph de Lisle passed his final examination and obtained his certificate as lieutenant, thus bringing the first half of his naval career to an honourable close, his time was spent principally in various cruises on board the Flying Squadron, the intervals being devoted to periods of necessary study in connection with his profession, and to keenly appreciated visits to his home and family.

In the last week of May, 1876, he joined the *Sultan* at Spithead, and went out in her to meet H.M.S. *Pallas*, to which he had been appointed. The history of the next five years, up to February, 1884, when he sailed for Alexandria, is contained chiefly in letters written by himself. From these letters our space forbids us to quote, as we would otherwise gladly do. This brief record being, moreover, intended rather to furnish a portrait of Lieutenant de Lisle's Character and virtues, than to follow in detail the external events of his life, we must refer to our readers, should they desire a fuller acquaintance with these, to the interesting and ably arranged Memoir we owe to Mr. Oxenham's pen. The letters, besides being eminently characteristic, show their writer to have been a close and discriminating observer both of men and things, and are full of intelligent remarks respecting the various quarters of the globe which he visited by turns in the course of his various cruises, these being principally in the Mediterranean, on the Mexican or South American coast, and amid the islands of the Pacific. Over and over again he shows how religion was ever present with him, by the manner in which he notes any incident which jarred on his religious sense, and the pain he expresses when brought face to face with that *corruption optimi* in reference to Catholic discipline and morality, which is, unfortunately, to be met with in some parts of South America. His faith was too firmly rooted to be shaken, his ideas as to right and wrong were too well defined to be obscured or even blurred; but it is easy to gather that, brought up as he had been, the shock to him as both unexpected and severe. With just indignation he tells how he found the 'Holy Sacrifice made into a sacrilege', and how, in another place, where numerous interments had been made in the aisles of a cathedral, he noticed with grieved astonishment the words 'legitimate son of So-and-so' inscribed on some of the grave stones, legitimate birth being so rare as to constitute an honourable distinction worthy of being recorded!

We have seen how thorough and consistent was the piety of Lieutenant de Lisle in his early years, and the bright promise of that radiant morning was indeed abundantly fulfilled, so that when his brief career came to a premature close, and he was cut off in the strength and splendour of his manhood, he might well have made his own the words of the Apostle, *Servavi fidem*. Nor let us forget how much self-sacrifice and self-denial the consistent practice and open profession of his faith must have cost him, and how very difficult a thing it was to remain a pious and sincere Christian when his lot was cast, not amid the consecrated associations and edifying examples to be met with in his home, but among scenes where the influences were of an opposite tendency, and in the presence of companions who would fain have cast contempt alike upon his ancient faith and his chivalrous adherence not only to its principles, but to its practice also!

Ever humble and modest, his virtue was totally devoid of that unfortunate self-consciousness which mars the attractiveness and destroys the charm, even if it does not obliterate the merit, of many actions in themselves laudable and good. His self-depreciation was genuine and sincere, he meant what he said, and expressed in all simplicity his real opinion of himself. This frame of mind shows itself alike in small things and in great, in the omission from his letters of any of his own exploits, in the half-playful manner in which he speaks of being 'made to feel quite small' during his stay on board the *Sultan*, through his inability to play any instrument, never even alluding to the value in which his comrades held his vocal powers, these latter being of a high order, though he thought little of them himself, as he also did of his skill as a draughtsman, albeit his proficiency in this respect was of no mean kind. In reference to graver matters, the following extract form a letter written when he was only sixteen, after receiving the tidings of his brother Osmund's death, will speak for itself.

> I hope for the future, myself, I shall not be any more trouble to you, for this has been a new and bitter example, which has really brought me to myself. Would to God I had had such a blameless life as he; although I have not committed the most deadly sins, yet I must say my language is nothing like so good as it might be. However, from the day I heard the news (yesterday), just as I was going to a ball, a new leaf has been turned over.

Resolutions were, upon his lips, no mere empty words, but determinations to be adhered to and carried out into every-day life, and he was far too wise not to know, that those who content themselves with doing as little as possible are in imminent danger of coming ere long to omit even that little. Hence he was no minimizer, whether as to belief or practice, but ever strove, in a spirit of generosity, to do as much as he could. Whenever, he had the opportunity of being present at Mass, he invariably appeared early, and, out of respect to the Holy Sacrifice, made a point of attending in full uniform, and would go to Benediction also whenever it was possible for him to do so. Quite incidentally he mentions in one of his early letters how he had been fasting from six o'clock on Saturday evening until after twelve on Sunday, intending to receive Holy communion, but the weather proved too rough to allow of landing, and he had to defer it until the next week. During the last few years of his life, he made it a rule to abstain from smoking, of which he was very fond, during Lent and on all fast-days. This act of self-denial will be appreciated by all smokers; indeed, the venerated Bishop of Birmingham said in reference to it: 'That is what I call a fine action, for many people are capable of brave actions, who will never deny themselves a pleasure; a young man who does that will always keep straight.'

No one who has read this far, will be surprised to hear how devout a client of our Blessed Lady was Lieutenant de Lisle. The last time he was in England, his sister, Mrs Strutt, wishing to give him a really nice present, requested him to mention something he would like to have, and he asked for a strong rosary, as his own was so often breaking, begging that the crucifix attached to it might be indulgenced for the hour of death. This rosary he constantly wore round his neck, together with his highly-prized Scapular, and that glorious Mother, who never forgets her faithful children, procured for him the privilege of making on the eve of the great feast of the Immaculate Conception the Communion which proved to be his last, and of hearing Mass, also for the last time, on the festival itself. But of all this we shall have more to say when we come to speak of the fatal Nile expedition, upon which he started on the feast of the Assumption, a fact he fails not to note, adding: 'We are starting on a good day.'

We have already spoken of his splendid courage, and it is no exaggeration to say, that never was there any one to whom might more fitly be applied the words which the French poet puts into the mouth of one of his heroes:

Je crains Dieu, cher Abner, et n'ai point d'autre crainte.

And he was no less tender than brave, for the warmth of his affections – especially his devoted love for his mother – is one of the most striking features of his biography. Though so seldom at home, his interest in all which went on there was unflagging, and his sympathy, ever ready alike in sorrow and in joy, the pertinent and appreciative remarks which abound throughout his letters, affording ample proof of this. While speaking on this subject, we cannot refrain from expressing our opinion that Mr. Oxenham has read into one of Lieutenant de Lisle's letters his own opinion on a point which has long been, and still is, a disputed point among some Catholics. From his words to his sister respecting her young boy, that 'He will be ten times the fellow after having been at Eton or Harrow,' is inferred a preference for the system of the Protestant public schools as compared with that generally pursued at Catholic Colleges. This certainly was not Lieutenant de Lisle's opinion, as those who knew him most intimately can bear witness, and the above quoted words to his sister were merely intended to help her to make the best of the prospect before her, of being forced to send her son to Eton, for like a wise man he invariably strove to look on the brighter side of things, and these consoling words were written with this view, and never intended to convey the meaning assigned to them.

Kind he ever was to his family and friends, but his kindness did not stop here. It extended itself, on the contrary, to those who were hostile to him, and the following instance of this deserves to be recorded.

> There was a sailor who, from some which or perversity of temper, conceived a violent hatred of him, and showed it on all occasions by insulting and annoying him and refusing obedience to his orders. After quietly enduring his insolence for some time Rudolph called the man one day and pointed out to him that if a formal complaint were lodged with the authorities he was liable to be shot for disobedience, adding, however, that he would freely forgive him if he would try and do better for the future. The poor sailor was so overcome by this unexpected forbearance that Rudolph had thenceforth no more attached or obedient follower (p. 131).

It is not wonderful that his men were attached to an officer who, moreover, never spared himself, nor imposed any task he was not ready himself to discharge. On one occasion, during the Nile expedition, when a boat was carried away, he exposed himself to great risk and physical suffering, in order to recover it, and thus save his men from being blamed for its loss; and when only a midshipman, he willingly incurred the anger of his captain by allowing a mast, laden with sail, to fall overboard and be lost during the night in the height of a storm, rather than send a man up to reef the sail at the imminent peril of his life. Yet he knew how to be firm as well as kind, and to make his subordinates implicitly obey him. For instance, one day 'they got to church late, when the Mass was partly over, and on their beginning to move at the end he stopped them, saying they had not fulfilled their obligation, but must stop for another Mass, and they quietly complied.' This is no solitary instance, he was ever the most solicitous as to the spiritual interests of his men, and when there was no Mass to go to, he would collect them in his cabin, read the prayers and a sermon, or sometimes make an exhortation himself. 'He used to say laughingly that he could preach pretty well, and might eventually become a priest.'

Lieutenant de Lisle always felt an intimate conviction that he was destined to fall in battle, and he liked the idea of dying in the discharge of duty. Amid all the bright cheerfulness of his sunny and buoyant disposition, and the varied enjoyment he found in his successful and congenial career there is not wanting evidence of a current of deeper and graver, if not sadder, thought. Many phrases and expressions might be cited to show that he early learnt to look at this world in the light of Eternity, and to estimate at their right value those things of time and sense which can never satisfy a soul cast in a mould so high as his. In the letters he wrote during the course of that ill-starred expedition, from which he was never to return alive, this minor key, if so we may term it, recurs more frequently, as if he felt himself drawing near the brink of that dark river, from the thought of which human nature cannot but shrink.

Yet his cheerfulness never deserted him, and the manner in which he makes light of the hardships, privations, sufferings, and miseries of every sort, which he in common with his companions had to bear, is beyond all praise, as is also the unvarying and unequalled courage and endurance with which he played to the very end, what he must have known to be a losing game. The narrative contained in his letters is both graphic and interesting, but the few scattered quotations to which want of space would unavoidably restrict us, could give no adequate idea of the whole, either as to the facts of the story, or the feelings of the writer, and we must therefore refer our readers, as we did on a former page, to the Memoir itself for further and fuller information.

One moment we may halt, on our way to the fatal field, to notice Lieutenant de Lisles' record of his thirty-first and last birthday, November 23, 1884. 'You will be glad,' he writes to his mother, in a letter dated Naval Camp, Gemai, 'to hear that I kept my birthday last Sunday as you would wish, for I went to Holy Communion, as did numbers of the Canadians. The altar was in a tent among the palm–trees, and the men all stood round in a semi-circle and sang, and very well too, different parts in unison; altogether a very picturesque sight.' Again he went to Confession and Holy Communion on Sunday, the 7th of December, as appears from a statement made by the Abbé Bouchard (the excellent French priest who ministered on those occasions), and received for the last time that Heavenly Food, in the strength of which he was to perform the solemn journey which lay before him, 'unto the Mount of God'.

The last letter he ever wrote was on January 13, 1885. It was dated from Gakdul, which had been reached after a four days' march across the desert, and did not arrive in England until three weeks after the telegram announcing his death at the battle of Abu Klea, on the morning of the 17th of January. On the evening of the 16th, just as the men were preparing their evening meal, the Arab fire suddenly opened upon them from a peak some 1200 yards in front, and it never ceased for five minutes together during that night, which for so many brave men was to be their last on earth, and the period of agonized suspense was rendered yet more dreadful by incessant noise on the part of their foes, who 'kept banging their battle-drums, and making,' says one who was present, 'a most execrable din'. It is strange that the same device should have been adopted by the Scotch Puritans, whose malignant cruelty rendered sleep impossible to the Jesuit Fathers, on the eve of their martyrdom, by means of the unintermittent crash of military music from dark to dawn.

By ten o'clock the next morning the enemy was in full attack, the brunt of the battle falling on the Heavy Camel Regiment and the Naval Brigade, and the onset of the great Arab horde striking like a tempest upon our men, who were outnumbered in a proportion of eight or nine to one, and sweeping like a wave over the place where the Gardner gun had stood. Two officers and six men of the Brigade sacrificed their lives defending it, one of the officers being Lieutenant de Lisle.

Thus he fell, pierced by more than fifty spears, gallantly fighting even to the end 'for God, for his country and for justice', proving himself in death, as he had ever shown himself in life, a worth descendant of his Crusader ancestor, Sire John de l'Ile, whose tomb he had noticed when in Cyprus amid the ruins of the Cathedral of Famagusta. Early on the morrow, a detachment of men was told off to bury the dead on the field of battle, and 'all the bodies of the slain, officers and men together, were hastily thrown into a common grave'.

As we stand in thought beside the last resting-place of Rudolph de Lisle, it is impossible that there should not mingle with our feelings of reverential affection, interest, and admiration, some measure of human regret, when we remember how distinguished a career would have been open to him in the future, and how high a place he might have attained in his country's service. But God knows best. It is not fur us 'to know the times or moments which the Father hath put in His own power'. Let us turn our eyes from the earth to heaven, and rejoice to think how great a reward our hero will receive at the hand of the King of kings on the day when the night of time shall give place to the radiant dawn of that eternity to which we all look forward, and in the light of which we ought to live.

Appendix IV

MEMORIAL PULPIT
ST HENRY & ST ELIZABETH, SHEERNESS, KENT

On Sunday 28 February 1886, at St Henry & St Elizabeth Roman Catholic Church, Sheerness, Kent, a pulpit and brass tablet, designed by F.A. Walters, was dedicated as a memorial to the Catholic men who died fighting in the Egyptian Campaign of 1882–1884 and the Sudan Campaign 1884–1885. Costing £200, the money was raised entirely by subscription from the men of the Royal Navy and Royal Marines.

The five niches of the octagonal stone pulpit bear the carvings of St Athanasius (patron saint of Egypt) and the symbols of the four Evangelists. Dividing the niches are six marble columns, each column supporting a kneeling angel bearing, respectively, the coat of arms of Pope Leo XIII, the Bishop of Southwark, Lieutenant Rudolph de Lisle, the Admiralty, and Egypt and the Sudan, with the dates of the corresponding campaigns. The accompanying brass tablet reads:

Of your charity pray for the souls of

Lieut. Rudolph E.M.P. de Lisle, R.N.

J. Williams, L:G: Seaman	E. Breen, Serjeant, R.M.L.I
J. Murray, L:G: Seaman	M. Carey, Corporal, R.M.L.I
T. O'Brien, A.B. Seaman	W. Walters, Private
J. O'Connor, A.B. Seaman	T. Paveley, Private
F. Hogan, A.B. Seaman	E. Mead, Private
P. Darragh, Writer	E. M. Card, Private

Of the Naval Brigade
Who gallantly fighting for Queen and Country
Fell in the Egyptian Soudan Campaigns 1882–1885
And in whose memory this tablet and pulpit were erected
By the Catholic Officers and Men of the Royal Navy and Marines
R.I.P.

Memorial pulpit, Church of St Henry and St Elizabeth, Sheerness, Kent, showing coat of arms of Lt. Rudolph de Lisle. (*Photograph: Saddleton of Sheerness, date unknown*)

Close-up of de Lisle coat of arms. (*Photograph: Saddleton of Sheerness, date unknown*)

Appendix V

ENGRAVING OF THE ABU KLEA BATTLE SITE, 17 JANUARY 1885

Engraving 'Officers of the Desert Column before Abu Klea'. Property of The Squire de Lisle. The circled figure is believed to be Lt. Rudolph de Lisle.

MEMORIAL CAIRN, ABU KLEA GRAVEYARD

Memorial tablet at Abu Klea battle site. Rudolph's name can be seen at the bottom left.

Bibliography

Alexander, M., *The True Blue: Col. Fred Burnaby (1842–1885)*, (London: R. Hart–Davis, 1957)
Asher, M., *Khartoum*, (London: Viking (Penguin), 2005)
Barthorp, M., *Blood–Red Desert Sand: Egypt & Sudan 1882–1898*, (London: Cassell & Co., 1984)
Beresford, Charles William de la Poer, Baron Beresford, *The Memoirs of Admiral Lord Charles Beresford*, 2 vols, (London: Methuen & Co., 1914)
Bleby, Lt. Cmr. A. L., *Victorian Naval Brigades*, (Caithness: Whittles Publishing, 2006)
Bradford, Sarah, *Disraeli* (New York: Stein Publishing, 1983)
Brooks, R., *Long Arm of Empire: Naval Brigades from the Crimea to the Boxer Rebellion*, (London: Constable & Co, 1999)
Butler, Sir W.F., *Campaign of the Cataracts*, (London: Sampson Low, Marston, Searle & Rivington, 1887)
Chenevix-Trench, C., *The Road to Khartoum: A Life of General Charles Gordon*, (New York: Dorset Press, 1979)
Churchill, W.S., *The River War: A Historical Account of the Reconquest of the Soudan,* (New York: Carroll & Graf, 2000)
Cordingly, David, *Cochrane: The Real Master and Commander* (Thomas Cochrane (1775–1860)), (London: Bloomsbury, 2007)
De Cosson, E.A., *Fighting the Fuzzy–Wuzzy: Days and Nights of Service with Sir Gerald Graham's Field Force at Suakin*, (London: Greenhill Books, 1990)
Elton, Lord, *General Gordon*, (London: Collins, 1954)
Elton, Lord, *Imperial Commonwealth* (London: Collins, 1945)
Featherstone, D., *Khartoum 1885: General Gordon's Last Stand*, (Connecticut: Praeger, 2005)
Gleichen, Count Arthur, *With the Camel Corps Up the Nile*, (Wakefield: EP Publishing Ltd, 1975)
Kitson, F., *When Britannia Ruled the Waves: The Heyday of the Royal Navy: The Life and Paintings of Vice Admiral Sir Henry Kitson KBE, CB, 1877–1952*, (Somerset: Halsgrove House, 2017)
MacLaren, R., *Canadians on the Nile 1882–1898*, (Vancouver: University of British Columbia Press, 1978)
Magnus, Sir P., *Kitchener: Portrait of an Imperialist*, (London: John Murray, 1958)
Manning, Capt. T.D. and Walker, Cdr. C.F., *British Warship Names* (London: Putnam, 1959)
Matthew, H.C.G., *Gladstone 1809–1898* (Oxford: Oxford University Press, 1997)
Neillands, R., *The Dervish Wars: Gordon & Kitchener in the Sudan 1880–1898*, (London: John Murray, 1996)
Nicoll, Fergus, *Gladstone, Gordon and the Sudan Wars: The Battle Over Imperial Intervention in the Victorian Age*, (Barnsley: Pen & Sword, 2013)
O'Brian, Patrick, *The Wine Dark Sea* (London: Harper Collins, 1993)
Oxenham, Rev. H.N., *Memoir of Lieutenant Rudolph de Lisle, R.N. Of The Royal Naval Brigade On the Upper Nile* (London: Chapman and Hall, 1886)
Preston, A., *In Relief of Gordon: Lord Wolseley's Campaign Journal of the Khartoum Relief Expedition 1884–1885*, (London: Hutchinson of London, 1967)
Proverbio, J.-I., *Le Troisieme Nil Roman*, (Paris: Edité par Lattes, 1990)
Slatin Pasha, Sir R., *Fire & Sword in the Sudan,* (London: Edward Arnold & Co., 1930)
Snook, Col. M., *Beyond the Reach of Empire: Wolseley's Failed Campaign to Save Gordon and Khartoum*, (London: Frontline Books, 2013)
Snow, Philip, *Best Stories of The South Seas* (London: Faber & Faber, 1967)
Symons, J., *England's Pride: Gordon Relief Expedition*, (London: Hamish Hamilton, 1965)
Vale, Brian and Cochrane, Admiral Lord, *Memoirs of a Fighting Captain* (London: Folio Society, 2005)
Verner, Capt. W., *Sketches in Sudan*, (London: R.H. Porter, 1886)
Verney, Capt. E.H., *The Last Four Days of the 'Eurydice'*, (Portsmouth: Griffon & Co., 1878)
Whitehouse, H., *Science v Pluck or Too Much for the Mahdi*, (Mansfield: Hardcover Designs, 1987)
Wingfield–Stratford, E., *The History of British Civilization*, 2 vols (London: G. Routledge, 1928)
Wilson, Sir C., *From Korti to Khartum*, (London: William Blackwood & Sons, 1885)
The Navy List, Corrected to 20th December 1868 (London: John Murray, 1869)
The Navy List, Corrected to 20th June 1884 (London: John Murray, 1884)

Index